THE
CANADIAN
MOUNTED

A TRIVIA GUIDE TO
PLANES, TRAINS & AUTOMOBILES

MARK LESLIE

Stark Publishing

Stark Entertainment
An Imprint of Stark Publishing
Waterloo, Ontario
www.starkpublishing.ca

Publisher's Note: This work is intended as a celebration of a modern classic film that the author adores, and of all the people involved in its production. It was compiled with the intention of offering fans of this John Hughes movie a collection of various trivia and insights as gathered from numerous sources.

The Canadian Mounted / Mark Leslie
October 2022

Print ISBN: 978-1-989351-63-5
eBook ISBN: 978-1-989351-64-2

DEDICATION

This one is for three awesome groups of people.

First, it's for you, dear reader, because you're likely as big a fan of the movie as I am. We are bound by that mutual love!

Second, it's for every single person involved in the creation of the film, with a huge thank you for all of the smiles, laughs, heart-warming tears, and entertainment your work continues to bring to countless people.

*And third, this book is **especially** for John Hughes and John Candy. I can't even begin to thank you both for all the great things your work brought into my life. The legacy of the gifts you shared lives so strong in mine and so many other hearts.*

TABLE OF CONTENTS

INTRODUCTION:

The most unique moments in life can come from the most unexpected tangents on the journey

It has happened to all of us at one time or another.

We have a simple plan of getting somewhere or accomplishing something. It's one of those many "point A to point B" things. And, if it were to go off the way we initially intended, it would be one of thousands of happenstance moments that pass us by and are forgettable.

But the universe has other plans for us.

And therein lies an event that may seem frustrating while we're living through it, but it becomes one of those unique stories we have in our quiver of tales that can be shared over the years at countless dinner parties and social gatherings.

Or it might even be a life-altering experience.

Cue Neal Page, an uptight advertising executive who lives in Chicago but travels a lot for work. All he wants is to get home to his family for Thanksgiving. It's the type of commute he has done hundreds of times. Home to cab to airport, then airport to cab to office meeting. Then, the same pattern repeated at the end of day or week, depending on the specific business in question. It's a regular routine.

Only, this time, when his flight ends up rerouted to Wichita, Page finds himself reluctantly partnering with Del Griffith, an obnoxious yet personable and loveable traveling salesman.

The two embark on a cross-country adventure that involves numerous modes of transportation, unexpected and hilarious mishaps, and an overall unforgettable "odd couple" style adventure.

Roger Ebert described *Planes, Trains and Automobiles* as "a screwball comedy with a heart." I describe it as a timeless classic that I've watched countless times over the years—at least once a year, if not more.

(And since I'm Canadian, with heavy influences from my US neighbors to the south, I most often enjoy this movie during both Canadian Thanksgiving in October and American Thanksgiving in November).

My son, who is eighteen at the time I'm writing this, has enjoyed the film with me many times over these most recent years. Despite him growing up in a far more digitally connected world than the 1987 setting of the film—Neal and Del didn't have mobile phones or apps; there was no Uber, video chat, or easily available GPS options—the movie still resonates with him just as much.

When my son and I embarked on a road trip in the summer of 2020 and experienced a series of delays and mishaps along the way, including an unfortunate break-down of the RV we'd rented, our memories of this movie actually helped. Despite the frustration of the delay that meant arriving home twenty-four hours later than intended, we joked about a few similarities of our misadventure. Also, in the middle of our situation, we snapped a photo that was a nod to Neal and Del sitting outside the Braidwood Inn.

But I haven't just bonded with my son over this film. It's one of those movies I can talk about with friends both old and new. I'm pretty sure that one of the early "connecting factors" of someone I now count as a dear friend was a mutual love of the movie. The minute a line from this film came up in conversation, we both lit up and the discussion became far more animated. Julie Strauss and I have been close friends ever since, and even co-authored *Lover's Moon*, a paranormal romantic comedy together in May 2022.

That's the effect this movie can have.

In the same way that Neal Page and Del Griffith connected in a meaningful way, I'm positive that countless others have leveraged their love and passion for this movie to bond together.

I also suspect that you, dear reader, picked this book up because you hold the movie *Planes, Trains and Automobiles* in a similar high regard.

This book, which is being released for the 35th Anniversary of the film's release, is a playful, deeper and longer look at the John Hughes classic staring John Candy and Steve Martin. And that look is, of course, filtered through a lifelong fan's eyes.

It's an exploration and appreciation of the movie with a generous helping of adoration and respect. There's an overview of the film itself as well as scatterings of trivia and anecdotes. And yes, I know, as Neal Page says, that not everything is an anecdote. I did my best to discriminate and to choose ones that are funny or mildly amusing and interesting. I may even have found some that might be amusing accidentally.

But as I said, I'm sure that, if you've picked up this book, you likely have some sort of affinity or passion about *Planes, Trains and Automobiles*.

And I truly hope that you enjoy this retrospective journey through the film as much as I have enjoyed collecting this information to share with you.

The Author and his son waiting for their ride after being stuck on a highway in mid-Northern Ontario in the summer of 2020. The shot was a nod to the image of Neal and Del sitting on the trunk outside the Braidwood Inn

LOVE IS NOT A BIG ENOUGH WORD

A look at the film we love

Planes, Trains and Automobiles was released on November 25, 1987, the day before American Thanksgiving.

If you're wondering why I specified "American" Thanksgiving, it's because I'm Canadian, and we celebrate Thanksgiving on the second Monday in October. I like to think that us polite Canadians are just "warming" up the holiday season for our American neighbors.

The movie, which was produced on a $15 million dollar budget, and filmed over 85 days, grossed a little more than $7 million on its first weekend, and $49.5 million by the end of its twelve-week American run. While respectable, it was not considered a blockbuster. But it received much praise and acclaim, with many critics not only celebrating the on-screen chemistry of John Candy and Steve Martin, but its representation of a branching out from Hughes' previous teen comedies like *Ferris Bueller's Day Off*, *The Breakfast Club*, and *Sixteen Candles*.

And, like a fine wine or barrel-aged whisky, that acclaim, praise, and adoration grew in the minds and hearts of fans. It became a perennial holiday season classic, along with films like *It's a Wonderful Life* and *A Christmas Story*.

Hughes, would, of course, also launch two other films that are still celebrated and watched annually by countless fans: 1990's *Home Alone* and *National Lampoon's Christmas Vacation* which was released in 1989.

Like many other classics, *Planes, Trains and Automobiles* is a film that older generations enjoy introducing and passing along. My son and I have long watched the movie together at least once per year and consider it an important father/son tradition.

Part of the film's ongoing success is often attributed to how this humorous buddy movie comedy is delivered with sentimentality and authenticity.

As Jason Diamond wrote in his 2016 book *Searching for John Hughes*, it's a master class in the buddy comedy. "Martin and Candy turn in a great duel-comedic performance, two of the best ever working together at the peak of their powers," Diamond writes. "But they aren't why *Planes, Trains and Automobiles* is the one movie I've always gone back to year after year. The real reason why the film remains so beloved to me is simple: John Hughes wrote, directed, and produced the movie. That is what sets it apart and makes it special."

There was something quite unique when Hughes was involved in a movie in more than one of the top creative roles. In an interview clip from the "John Hughes for Adults" special feature on the 2009 "THOSE AREN'T PILLOWS!" Edition DVD of the movie, Hughes explained that he set *The Breakfast Club* in a single location because he needed a lower budget film executives would take a chance on letting him direct.

That film, which was shot on a budget of $1 million grossed $51.5 million and is often considered one of the writer and director's finest and most memorable works.

Hughes was known for being a very fast writer, typing out scripts at a lightning-fast pace.

He explained, in the special feature "Getting There is Half the Fun: The Story of *Planes, Trains and Automobiles*" that when he sets out to write a script, he tries to get it done as soon as possible to see if he liked the idea. Then he would go through maybe twenty-five to thirty re-writes.

And that re-writing process wouldn't finish until the final cut of the film, which he always does at the last minute.

Hughes explains that the film script is not the finished work, but "it's just a blueprint."

Michael McKean, who played the role of the State Trooper in the film, expresses, in that same special feature, that he appreciated Hughes' manner of directing one of his scripts, never holding the script up as a precious text that could not be adapted and adjusted during filming.

Hughes was inspired to write the script for *Planes, Trains and Automobiles* after a trip where he left Chicago for New York, intending to come back the same day. But his flight was diverted to Wichita, Kansas, and it took him five days to get home.

The first draft of the script was written in three days. By that time in his career most of his first drafts would take anywhere between three and five days.

In my researching scripts from this film, I was able to get my hands on PDF scans of two different ones.

The first was a May 5, 1986, script with the title of "REVISIONS." The second was titled "Final Shooting Script" and dated June 23, 1987.

What I found particularly intriguing about the scripts after reading through them both numerous times, was how many scenes in the final film were so different from that "final shooting" script. In some cases, there were scenes that appeared in the 1986 version that were not in the "final" 1987 version that still made it into the film.

I suppose this further shows what both Hughes and McKean expressed about the writer/director continuing to adjust and adapt the script all the way up to the very final moment in production.

According to various sources associated with screenwriting, the average screenplay script runs anywhere between 90 to 120 pages.

The May 1986 version of the script I was able to find is close to that at 129 pages. But the "final shooting script" from June 1987 runs a whopping 165 pages.

It is believed that John Hughes shot over 600,000 feet (or 180,000 meters) of film for this movie. That length is almost twice the industry average.

This obviously gave Hughes, and film editor Paul Hirsch a significant amount of material to cut down

Hirsch shared that the original cut of the movie clocked in at three hours and forty minutes. He worked with John Hughes to edit it down to two hours.

That two-hour version was test screened, and it was most likely used to produce trailers for the film, which is why the trailers include several deleted scenes (such as Del doing an Elvis impersonation in a hotel washroom, Neal eating pizza, and the two of them talking about Don Ho in the burned-out car). The movie was edited another time to bring it down to one hour and thirty-three minutes for the theatrical release.

Hirsch has shared that apparently, that two-hour version of *Planes, Trains and Automobiles* still exists, but he isn't sure exactly where it is.

There was even a rumored three-hour version of the film. Although that one apparently is not in order. It's allegedly a mess of footage that would take "months, maybe even years" according to Hughes to transform into an actual film. It is locked away in a Paramount vault, and according to Hughes, most of it has probably deteriorated over the years.

One of the reasons there was likely so much footage was that Hughes enjoyed making films in a very collaborative process. He often challenged the actors to add their own improvisational elements to each performance, and after a successful take, tell them to do it one more time, but to change it up a bit.

"Every take was a little bit different," Hughes said in an interview about *Plane, Trains and Automobiles.* "There's no point in doing the same take over and over and over."

Before they started working on a scene, Hughes would enjoy having a brief conference with the people involved to see if there was any way to stage it better.

"I don't care where an idea comes from. "If I think of it, or whoever," Hughes said. "I welcome it."

It's clear in all the research I've done about the making of this film, that Hughes consistently did that throughout.

And it's that complex collaborative efforts which allows the movie and the people in it to shine in so many ways.

THE PROP BOOK

The real book that became a prop book, that became a real book

I'm sure that, in at least one way, shape, or form, the cover of this book caught your eye.

If you're a book nerd like me, or perhaps just someone who has seen the movie countless times, you might have recognized it immediately as the book that Del Griffith is reading when Neal and Del bump into one another at the New York airport where they're both flying to Chicago.

I have long been a lover of books so, whenever a book appears in a scene in a television show or movie, I pay attention to it. I want to know if it's a real book, and, if it is, what the book is. What is that fictional character reading? And why did the writer/director place that book in the scene?

In this case, as Neal Page sits across from Del Griffith in the airport, recognizing him as the guy who "stole" his cab on Park Avenue earlier that afternoon, Del is reading a paperback book.

The book is *The Canadian Mounted*, which looks to be a pornographic mass market paperback. I became familiar with that genre of novels when I started working in the book industry in 1992. There was an entire section of wall filled with erotic fiction, mostly mass produced in those pocket-sized editions at the front of the fiction wall in the first bookstore I worked at.

While some of the books had author names on them, many of them were attributed to "Anonymous." We nicknamed that sub-section of fiction the Anonymous Section. That bookstore was a Coles on Sparks Street in Ottawa, Ontario. The location, which was two levels—*a large street level shop, then an entire basement level filled with discounted and remaindered books*—closed in 1993. But during my time there, we sold thousands of copies of those "Anonymous" pocketbooks (also cheekily referred to as "one-handers") to plenty of people, many likely traveling salespeople like Del Griffith.

I always suspected that the title of this fake prop book was a nod to actor John Candy's citizenship.

In the original script the first time Neal looks across at Del in the airport in New York, Del has a cigarette in his mouth and a cardboard food box with a pair of jumbo hot dogs in it and is applying mustard to the dogs. Later, when Neal looks over, Del is described as being in stocking feet, chomping on a toothpick and reading a pornographic novel. While reading he inserts a baby finger into one ear and violently twists it around.

Later, when they're on their flight from New York to Chicago, Del partially explains the book. "I'm just happy to have someone to talk to," Del says in the original script. "I finished my book about an hour ago. Filthy goddarn thing. When you travel as much as I do, you run out of reading material. If it's been published, I've read it. Fiction, non-fiction, the classics—Robbins, Krantz, Iacocca. You name it, I've read it. I got so hard-up last week on a layover in Atlanta, I read a biography of Prince. That's not his real name, by the way, It's Rogers Nelson."

I'm far from the only one fascinated by this prop book that appears very briefly in the film. There has been plenty of chatter in online forums over the years regarding it.

Canadian actor Ryan Reynolds—who has produced tributes to John Candy and often speaks of his adoration of John Candy and the movie *Planes, Trains and Automobiles*—was instrumental in the subtle nod to Candy that appeared in *Deadpool 2.*

In a May 2022 interview with David Letterman on Season 4, Episode 4 of *My Next Guest Needs No Introduction* Reynolds spoke about that nod.

"Growing up, I had a real obsession, quite genuinely, with John Candy. And I still do," Reynolds told Letterman. "Steve Martin, a lot of the guys that came out of *SNL.*

"If I'm flummoxed in a scene or I can't figure out a way in, I will just copy them. That sort of Neal Page, *Planes, Trains and*

Automobiles, kind of aggressively unimpressed, kind of over-it character. I just love that; I can never get enough.

"It's supposed to be this non-fiction soft porn, basically," the Canadian actor said. "One of those sorts of trash, way sub-Danielle Steel. We're talking nasty. He reads it in *Planes, Trains and Automobiles*. And I have that book. Not the exact one he's holding but I had it remade for *Deadpool*."

Reynold's character Wade Wilson can be seen holding that replica book in the superhero film.

It has been pointed out, by observant fans that a still image of Wade Wilson reading the prop version of *The Canadian Mounted* shows the way he is holding the book in his left hand—including the finger placement of the index and middle fingers on the front/outside of the book, and the thumb, ring finger and little fin-ger in the back/inside part of the book —is the same way Del holds the book in that airport scene.

Screen shot from Planes, Trains and Automobiles *of Steve Martin (Neal Page) and John Candy (Del Griffith) with Del reading the book.*

[This scene this screen shot is from did not make it into the final film cut. In the movie, Del is reading the book sitting across from Neal at LGA]

Screen shot from a Ryan Reynolds Instagram Story

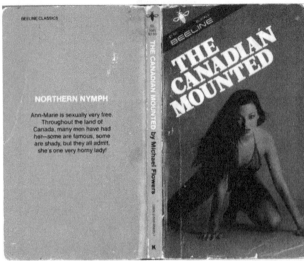

Scan of a copy of the original THE CANADIAN MOUNTED

If, like me, you have studied or at least looked closely at frozen screen images of John Candy and Ryan Reynolds holding that prop book, you'll notice the slight differences in the original verses the replica.

- In the original, the model on the cover is wearing a blue bikini. In the 2018 edition, the model is wearing a bikini that appears to be a potentially floral pattern of dark green and grey. She is also wearing a necklace adorned with "shark-tooth" shapes and a pair of thick metal bracelets

- The John Candy version of the book is the size of a typical mass market sized edition (which usually run 4.25 X 6.87 inches), but the Ryan Reynolds version appears to be a taller and thinner styled book. I'm guessing the dimensions to be 4.25 X 8.25. (Don't judge me. I'm a gigantic book nerd, and trim sizes and binding are important aspects of the industry).

- The pose of the model in the original version has her left arm extended with her hand to the ground in front of her leg. The pose that the model in the later version of the book takes has her left hand held up with her hand on the side of her face or perhaps her neck beneath her hair

When creating this book, I was limited to the available trim sizes with the type of printing (POD—Print on Demand) I used.

But the size I used is close to the original with a trim size set at 7 X 4.25 inches.

In addition, prior to hearing from a well-researched fan of John Hughes (I'll talk about them later), my cover designer and I weren't able to find a model in the exact same pose.

The original cover planned for this book would have been a third alteration of the same theme.

We both looked through hundreds of different stock images from multiple licensing platforms, and I ended up purchasing a few different ones.

I also debated about the possibility of trying to mimic the replica version used in *Deadpool* rather than the original but decided it would be best to honor the original book Del Griffith was holding as close as possible.

The closest in "look" to the original model still didn't have the right leg and arm positions, so we set about in Dr. Frankenstein fashion leveraging bits from different models, and also manipulated the positioning of her limbs.

A mockup text-less cover using one of the models that had similar hair and close to the correct limb positioning

A raw stock image with one of the blonde models in a similar pose

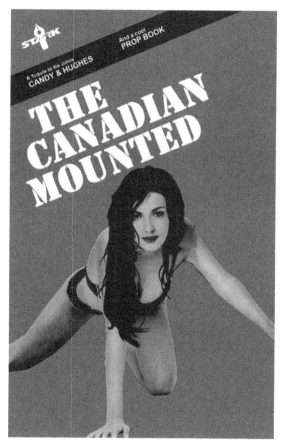

The original concept for the front cover for this book, leveraging a combination of models, with different hair and limb configuration

By the end of the creation of the original mockup, Juan Padron, my cover designer, and I had something that I felt could be pulled off.

I also tried to replicate the "look" of the text from the original cover, but with my own custom text and imagery.

I used the quill from my Stark Publishing logo and re-adapted that logo to match the indistinguishable logo that seemed to appear on that original cover, and then added text about it being a tribute to a prop book.

It was similar enough for fans to "recognize" it from the cover image and the title. (The way fans recognized Ryan Reynolds' replica version from the *Deadpool* movie).

I then prepared the pre-order for online bookstores and continued my research for this book. (*Interestingly, despite this book including a respectable number of trivia, anecdotes, and other related material, I did have to eventually stop adding details, as I wanted the page count of this book to closely match the page count of the original book*).

In March of 2022, I received a message via an online form on my website. It was from someone who identified themself as Five Seventeen. That note was a significant game-changer in this project.

The first line of the multi-paragraph message to me read:

Hi Mark, I came across your blog (It being the anniversary of John Candy's death) and wanted to let you know that THE BOOK IS REAL.

That email, the details included, and the following correspondence, was a significant and important discovery that I am extremely appreciative for.

Because ultimately, it led to an insight that people have speculated about for a long time.

And that's what we'll explore in more detail in the next chapter.

THE REAL BOOK
The original THE CANADIAN MOUNTED

The Canadian Mounted was long rumored to have been a prop book, likely used as a cheeky nod to the Canadian actor John Candy by the prop team working on the John Hughes film.

I even had my pre-order of this book live, with a description decreeing that, for the first time, the infamous prop book would become a *real* book. (I suppose I thought this might be a *Pinocchio* moment—helping it finally become a real book the way the wooden doll dreams of becoming a real boy in the classic 1883 novel by Italian author Carlo Collodi and most notably known from the 1940 Disney film).

That's when I received a note via the contact form on my author website. The person identified themself as Five Seventeen. They'd run a John Hughes themed podcast for several years called PRETTY IN PODCAST and had done a lot of research about the director and his many projects.

Five Seventeen had found a blog post of mine in which I was talking about this project; they wanted to ensure I knew that it was, in fact, a real book, and shared several details with me about it.

The Canadian Mounted was published in 1981 by Bee-Line books. It was written under the pseudonym Michael Flowers using ISBN 0-503-05690-1.

Here are some interesting notes about that book's ISBN. (*See, I told you I was a gigantic book nerd*). 13-digit ISBNs weren't introduced until the late 1990s because so many books were being printed that Bowker (the agency responsible for creating and selling them to publishers) was going to run out. All 10-digit ISBNs were converted to 13-digit Bookland EAN codes (these were used for UPC codes often printed on the back of books for scanning at the cash register). Conversion to the 13-digit number is done by dropping the final number, which is a check-digit, adding 978 to the front, then re-calculating a new check digit. They were running out of 978 codes (*the book world's version of the "Y2K Bug"*) and needed to convert to 13-digit codes by adding the prefix of 979 to "Bookland." The 13-digit ISBN for this book would be 978-0-503-05690-2.

The book was printed in the United States and had a retail price printed on it (in the top left-hand corner of the cover on the black diagonal banner) of $2.50. The other text appearing on the original cover were "BEELINE" in a larger font, and, in the same size text size as the price, the catalog reference number of "BL5690-V." (The 5690 is part of the "registrant element" of the ISBN code).

The barely distinguishable white logo above that black banner is a bee. On other titles from the same publisher, the bee logo wasn't a monochromatic white, but was black with the transparent eyes, wings and stripes filled in with yellow.

The spine contains the same logo, but in black, and with the text BL, 5690, and $2.50 on separate lines below that at the top. The book's title appears at a 180° angle followed by "by Michael Flowers" (the author's name does not appear on the front cover). Below that, also at 180° is the ISBN. And below that a capital K.

The back cover has "BEELINE CLAS-SICS" on the top left in small black text, the heading "NORTHERN NYMPH" centered with a black, smaller text six-line description below it. There is no bar code on the back cover.

The text on the back of the book is:

NORTHERN NYMPH

Ann-Mare is sexually very free.
Throughout the land of
Canada, many men have had
her—some are famous, some
are shady, but they all admit,
she's one very horny lady!

Beeline Classics were an imprint of Carlyle Communications, Inc. of New York. Bee-Line Books was started in 1964 by David Zentner.

Sometime in the spring of 1981 Bee-Line published their last book—it is possible that *The Canadian Mounted* may have been one of their last published titles, and was not registered for copyright—and on April 22, 1987 they filed for bankruptcy.

THE MISSING OXFORD COMMA
The missing comma from the movie's title, plus the extraneous plurals

The movie *Planes, Trains and Automobiles* is one I consider almost perfect in every way.

One exception, of course, is the missing comma in the title of the film.

The Oxford comma, which is often also referred to as the serial comma, is the last comma in a list of items. It has been a long-time topic of debate among scholars and grammar afficionados. And the debates center around whether the use of that comma in a list reduces or creates ambiguity in a statement.

Those in favor of the serial or Oxford comma would state that the movie's title should be *Planes, Trains, and Automobiles* as it lists three of the main ways Neal and Del travel in their multi-day misadventure road trip.

The arguments arise because placement of commas can change the meaning of a sentence.

For example, consider this sentence, expressed from Neal Page's point of view:

- *On my way to Chicago, I encountered Del Griffith, a traveling salesman and a blabbermouth.*

This sentence describes Del Griffith as a salesman and a blabbermouth.

But what if a serial or Oxford comma were introduced?

- *On my way to Chicago, I encountered Del Griffith, a traveling salesman, and a blabbermouth.*

Use of that serial comma makes it sound as if Neal was traveling with three people. One of them was named Del Griffith, the other was a traveling salesman, and the third one was a blabbermouth.

Is the missing comma in the movie title an oversight, or was it purposefully left out?

Could it have been left out by Hughes just for the purposes of simplification? Perhaps an additional comma in the title might clutter it up.

Or maybe the movie title denotes that the travel in the film happens on planes, and then it also happens on trains and automobiles. As in two distinct modes of transportation: one is air travel, and the others are ground transportation.

Of course, Neal and Del only travel on a single airplane and a single train, not multiple airplanes and trains—unless you count the subway ride in Chicago a train. The plural automobiles reference is far more accurate since they travel in numerous automobiles: taxis, a pick-up truck, a bus, and a transport truck.

There is one other clue I uncovered to determine why there appears to be a "missing" Oxford comma in the title.

Reading through the "final script" Hughes wrote, I noticed a consistent pattern of him *not* employing the Oxford comma in places where I would have used them.

So perhaps this was his style or chosen preference. Particularly since he wrote scripts that you weren't meant to see, merely enjoy when adapted into film. I can imagine, from his perception, the script was a tool, or a loose blueprint to help directors and actors adapt in their own unique way. If there were missing commas, or even minor spelling errors in a script, who really cared. This medium was meant to be enjoyed on a screen, not on a page.

Regardless of where you stand on the Oxford comma debate, or whether the movie title *should* have a serial comma in it, I'm sure you would agree that doesn't take away in any way, shape, or form (see what I did there?) from the brilliance of the film itself.

TRIVIA

Anecdotes and chosen things that are funny, mildly amusing, or interesting

I uncovered numerous trivial notes about this movie revealed in various interviews with people involved in the film.

Others came from articles and dedicated fans who have posted them in online forums.

The following, compiled roughly in the order of scenes from the movie, includes many of them—presented for your enjoyment or perhaps anecdotal sharing.

- Roger Ebert the movie critic gave *Planes, Trains and Automobiles* three and a half out of 4 stars in his original 1987 review of the film. In 2000, for a follow up review, he gave it four out of four stars, and it was also included in his list of "Great Movies." Ebert allegedly watched the movie almost every Thanksgiving.

- Had Neal and Del stuck around at the airport in Wichita, they very likely would have made it back to Chicago in time. A scene cutting over to Neal's house has his wife Susan watching the news which shows that O'Hare airport is clearing up. But where would the fun be if they'd just done that?

- Understandably so, no existing transportation company wanted to appear deficient or inept in any way within the context of the movie. This meant that film crews had a significant amount of work to do to replicate companies and transportation props. They had to build an entire set that looked like an airline terminal, refurbish old railroad cars, rent up to twenty miles of railroad track, design a rental car company logo and uniforms, and also rent about two hundred and fifty cars for Neal Page's infamous Rent-a-Car sequence.

- John Candy's role in the film required him to have a moustache and a perm. Instead of wearing a fake moustache (which, in previous films, bothered him because people were always pressing his face to ensure the glued moustache was lying flat) he grew one. And his hair was permed at Crimpers Haircutters in Buffalo, New York.

- Some network TV versions of the movie include an alternate version of the scene where Neil confronts the woman at the car rental counter (but with all instances of the f-word removed). Additionally, there have been TV versions that show the deleted "Airplane Food" scene. This scene appears in the special features of some of the DVD and Blu Ray releases of the movie. It takes place during the New York to Chicago plane ride with Neal and Del having dinner on the plane. Del talks about the various meals he orders on different airlines. Neal's dinner is a lasagna, which due to various delays, has been reheated multiples times and is barely recognizable. Neal offers his food to Del, who shares it with the old man next to Neal. Neal decides to keep the brownie with his meal, but a woman in the seat in front of him flips her hair back over the seat and onto his brownie, disgusting Neal. So, he gives the brownie to Del.

- As the movie and title sequence opens, the sound effects heard are of planes, trains, and automobiles, in exactly that order.

- The "final shooting script" of June 1987 contains more than a full page describing the meandering fall of a single snowflake from the clouds, past a commercial airliner, over a set of commuter railroad tracks, and then a car, and finally down to what is likely the Page household. The end of the snowflake scene states: "CUT ON JARRING BLEAT OF AN AUTOMOBILE." It then cuts to the outside of Neal's office building in New York, a high-level view of the crowded New York streets, then quick snapshots of various people that help set this "beginning of the holiday season" time setting.

- John Candy isn't the only Canadian actor in the film. Among them are Lynman Ward, who, uncredited, plays John, Neal Page's colleague who infamously tells him "You'll never make the 6:00." Lyman not only played the father of the title character in Hughes' *Ferris Bueller's Day Off*, but also appeared in the Hughes film *She's Having a Baby*, also uncredited.

- Neal's "Del-related" delays took place well before the "stolen" taxi moment; at least according to a scene in the final shooting script. In it, as Neal gets out of the elevator on the main floor of the office building, he sees a huge crowd making progress through the front doors seemingly impassible. The script then cuts to "INT. LOBBY REVOLVING DOORS. DAY. Through the crowd we catch a glimpse of an old steamer trunk jammed in the revolving doors. An unseen person is struggling with it. WE DON'T SEE HIS FACE." It is obviously Del. And it's a parallel "unseen" person moment reminiscent of the stolen cab scene, where, as Neal is bartering with the lawyer for the cab, Del's trunk and his arms and hands are seen, but he isn't.

- Kevin Bacon, who plays Neal Page's nemesis taxi racer is the fifth-billed actor in the credits, despite only appearing in a brief scene at the beginning of the film with perhaps one minute of screen time.

- Bacon was brought into the film shortly after finishing work on the John Hughes film *She's Having a Baby*, which didn't come out until the following year. Bacon had mentioned to Hughes if he ever needed him all he had to do was to call. And so, Hughes did. Many fans have speculated that this cameo appearance by Bacon is as his lawyer character in *She's Having a Baby*. Another interesting note is the belief that this scene might be a nod to the 1986 movie *Quicksilver*, in which the character played by Bacon is racing someone on a bicycle.

- Bacon "sort of" appears again later in the film. When Neal phones his wife to tell her that he has been delayed again, she has the bedroom television on in the background. You can hear the fight from *She's Having a Baby* between the characters played by Kevin Bacon and Elizabeth McGovern, when she screams that she doesn't like his friend's girlfriend. It's "impossible" for her to be watching this movie on television, as *She's Having a Baby* was actually released in theatres 3 months later, in February 1988

- The trunk that Neal Page trips over is stamped with the following address: "Del O. Griffith C/O American Light Fixtures Shower Curtain Ring Division P.O. Box 60608 Chicago, IL.

- Del's name on the trunk (Del O. Griffith) means that his initials spell out the word DOG. Five months before the release of this film, John Candy appeared in the 1987 film *Spaceballs* in which he plays a half-man/half-dog character named Barf.

- According to John Thompson, a friend of John Candy, after filming, Del's trunk was kept in John's office in Brentwood and was used as a coffee table.

- Immediately after Del "steals" Neal's cab and the vehicle drives away, there is a shot of the empty space where the taxi used to be. If you look closely, you can see a shower curtain ring floating in the puddle near the curb.

- There's a scene from the final shooting script that shows Neal continuing to be held up in security and service counter lines by Del Griffith either asking for confirmation of his flight's special meal order or not realizing he'd walked through the security screen with a shoehorn stuck in his shoe. (This movie took place before it was mandatory to remove shoes as part of security screening for most flights)

- Neal and Del are on Mid-Central Airlines (a fictional airline company) Flight 909.

- Shots of the exterior of the New York to Chicago aircraft in flight come from a re-use of the 707 flying through the storm from the 1980 movie *Airplane!* Which was also released by Paramount Pictures.

- The old man who falls asleep on Neal Page's shoulder on the plane is played by Bill Erwin. Erwin also appeared in the John Hughes films *Home Alone* (1990) and *She's Having a Baby* (1988). In a deleted scene that appears in numerous special feature DVD and Blu-Ray discs, Erwin has a few speaking lines as a gentleman who is hard-of-hearing.

- The Wichita airport, which was the final one to feature extras during the filming process, was shot on a studio soundstage in Hollywood.

- When the airline employ in the Wichita airport scene announces that the flight has been cancelled, visible behind him is the word "nowhere" as the flight's destination.

- Ben Stein, the actor who played the airline employee announcing the cancelation was also in the 1986 John Hughes film *Ferris Bueller's Day Off* and played a monotone sleep-inducing economics teacher with the often-quoted lines of "Anyone? Anyone?" and "Bueller? Bueller?"

- The "Doobie's Taxiola" taxi scene was filmed on a stretch of road in Madison, Ohio. After filming that scene, John Hughes allegedly sent everyone home, keeping a small skeleton crew and the actors John Candy, Steve Martin and Larry Hankin, who played Doobie. As Hughes often did, he asked them to improvise in the cab and they spent an entire afternoon doing just that. According to an interview that Larry Hankin gave, a ten-minute short from the footage was made. Hankin was told by Chris Columbus that Hughes had showed the short film to him one afternoon.

- Neal and Del stay in a hotel in Wichita Kansas called the Braidwood Inn. The hotel was actually located in Braidwood, Illinois.

- When Neal and Del check into the Braid-wood, Gus, the clerk, has two flags on his counter. It's the American flag crossing the flag of the United States Air Force. Charles Tyner, who played Gus, served in the Army Air Forces, the predecessor of the U.S.A.F. in World War II. Also, McConnell Air Force Base is located in Wichita, Kansas.

- Neal and Del stay in room 114 of the Braidwood Inn.

- As he is settling into the hotel room, Del takes out a picture of his wife, Marie, who was played by Susan Issacs. (At this point in the film, of course, we do not realize that Marie is deceased). There were a few flashback scenes with Del and Marie that did not make it to the film. Only the picture of Susan, as Marie, made it in. John Candy, Susan Isaacs, and Dylan Baker (who played Owen) were reunited in the 1991 film *Delirious*. In both movies, the character played by Isaacs is called Marie.

- There were several scenes from the Braidwood Inn stay that did not appear in the movie but did show up in the trailer. One of them shows Del Griffith in the bathroom of the Braidwood Inn singing into a hairbrush while doing an impersonation of Elvis Presley as well as flossing.

- Steve Martin claimed, in an interview about the film, that the scenes at the Braidwood Inn, in particular the shower scenes where he was walking around on the wet tiles, led to him coming down with a case of athlete's foot.

- Another moment cut from the film but that appears in the trailer shows Neal Page seeming to struggle with a loaded slice of pizza in the hotel room. This comes from a sequence involving Del ordering pizza and beer. The reason for Neal's revulsion is that he'd asked Del to order him a salad, but they didn't have any. Instead, Del asked for extra vegetables on the pizza.

- In that same pizza sequence, Del tries to pay with a $100 bill, but the pizza boy doesn't have change. Del then uses money he takes from Neal's wallet (By then, he has inadvertently revealed to the delivery person that there are several larger bills in both their wallets) and only gives the delivery boy a $1 tip. In the script, the delivery boy returns to break into their room to rob them. The break-in, of course, still appears in the final cut of the film, but it appears to be a random burglar instead of a thief who knew what kind of cash they had.

- Finally, in that "pizza and beer" sequence, Del opens a beer after having left the six-pack on the vibrating bed. The beer sprays all over the bed sheets. Neal Page delivers a line later which does appear in the film's final cut that refers to this moment.

- When Del is annoyingly clearing his sinuses in the motel room, the pattern of deep nose noises he makes is to the tune of "Shave and a Haircut." It's the "two bits" response, after a pause, that sets Neal off on his tirade.

- The nasal passage clearing scene is also considered an ode to Felix Unger, who did the same in the 1968 movie *The Odd Couple.* That movie, starring Jack Lemon and Walter Matthau was about a similarly mismatched pair of friends living together.

- The speech John Candy gives after Neal's monologue about how having to have "been with Del Griffith" is parodied in an episode of *Family Guy*. ("Baby Not on Board" Season 7, Episode 4). In this 2008 episode, there's a moment where, after Lois chastises Peter, he recites that speech nearly verbatim.

- Filming of the "those aren't pillows!" scene took multiple takes. As the camera panned from the nightstand to the cuddling Del and Neal, actors Steve Martin and John Candy kept laughing in anticipation of their next actions and lines. Several takes were "ruined" by the similar anticipatory laughter of the camera crew, as the camera would "shake" with their laughs.

- After the two men jump out of bed in horror, Neal asks Del if he saw the Bears game last week. Del responds with: "Hell of a game" and "Bears got a great team this year...gonna go all the way." Thanksgiving fell on November 26th that year, 1987. The previous Bears game would have been Sunday the 22nd. In that game, the Bears beat Detroit in an impressive 30-10 victory. At the time, the Bears were 8-2, and on their way to an 11-4 season They did not, however, "go all the way." They lost 21-17 to the Washington Redskins (renamed in 2022 to the Washington Commanders) in the Divisional Round.

- If you've ever wondered how Neal and Del got out of the diner where, while having breakfast, they discovered they'd been robbed the previous night, it is explained in the final shooting script. A scene that didn't make it to the film shows Del trying to negotiate a deal on the breakfast by claiming he never got the oatmeal he ordered. After a bit of a back-and-forth with the waitress, and after she admits to pulling a hair out of his oatmeal "that'd make your arm pit proud," Del pretends to be with the Department of Agriculture. She ends up ripping up their check.

- *Planes, Trains and Automobiles* marked the film debut of Dylan Baker.

- Dylan Baker created the Owen character himself. He came up with the facial ticks, snorts, and goofy expressions all on his own. Lulie Newcomb, the actress who played his wife, said she found it extremely difficult to keep a straight face while filming that scene with him.

- Director John Hughes was well-known for encouraging improvisational moments with his actors. He was fond of how well that could help to capture a genuine reaction on film. Unsatisfied with the Owen scene introductions after several takes, Hughes privately instructed Dylan Baker to wipe spit in his right hand just before shaking hands with Neil Page. Steve Martin was not expecting this, and his disgusted reaction to shaking Baker's saliva slathered hand was real. The film crew reportedly exploded in laughter as Martin ran off to wash his hands immediately following the encounter. Hughes got the reaction he needed, and the footage was kept in the film.

- The rural train station, where Neal and Del buy the tickets for their ill-fated train ride, is the same station seen in the 1984 film *The Natural*. It is located in South Dayton, New York.

- John Hughes' original setting choice for the train station and platform was the station in Kankakee, Illinois, sixty miles south of Chicago. The cast and crew were in town for a week waiting for the weather to get cold enough to make snow, and during that time several interior scenes were filmed at an abandoned warehouse using a "cover set".

- Del Griffith's friend at the railroad, Bert Dingman, is a direct reference to Robert O. Dingman, Jr., President of the New York and Lake Erie Railroad, where the train scenes were filmed.

- The train that was used in the movie apparently still sits dormant and unused to this day at a small rural station in the Western New York town of Gowanda with the "Contrack" logos still present on the engine and cars.

- Jeri Ryan, who later became known for her roles in *Star Trek: Voyager* (Seven of Nine) and *Boston Public* (Veronica "Ronnie" Cooke) was an extra on the bus scene, but was fired for laughing. Ryan, who was nineteen years old at the time, could not stop laughing in response to Candy and Martin. Hughes had to fire her, and the scenes were re-shot without her.

- *Plane, Trains and Automobiles* is the second movie where John Candy plays a traveler

who gets on the nerves of a fellow passenger sitting next to him. This occurred
in the 1985 movie *Volunteers*. In addition,
the character Candy plays in that film also
leads a group of passengers in song. On
the Greyhound bus, Candy as Del leads
the other passengers in the 1960 "The
Flintstones" theme song. In *Volunteers* he
led the 1978 "Puff the Magic Dragon"
song on an airplane.

• After Del sells shower curtain rings at the
bus station by pretending they are earrings, Del and Neal go for a meal at a
nearby diner. In one shot of the two of
them sitting at their booth, a waitress and
female customer appear in the background wearing the shower curtain rings
as earrings.

• The outdoor scenes at Lambert Airport in
St. Louis were shot during winter, but the
weather was uncharacteristically warm (it
was apparently in the mid-eighties Fahr-
enheit). The crew had to truck in the snow
that appears in those scenes.

• Ken Tipton, an extra who met Candy
while working as his stand-in during the
St. Louis part of the movie's filming, cred-

its John Candy as a mentor who made a positive difference in his Hollywood career. In a frank conversation with Tipton, Candy shared that acting was hard work that requires a lot of practice and rehearsing. He said if Tipton was ever serious about his career to call Candy up. And, years later, when Tipton managed to get ahold of Candy, the Canadian actor mentored him in earning his SAG card.

- *Just in case you worry that I may have forgotten the infamous Marathon Car Rental scene, I didn't. There's an entire chapter (the very next chapter) dedicated to Neal's rant at the St. Louis airport car rental counter.*

- While the Marathon Car Rental scene was the single one-minute scene in the movie that led to its R rating, there was another scene cut from the film that would likely have tested the mostly "family friendly" film's rating level. In a 2012 interview with Joe Vannicola, actress Debra Lamb shared her experiences working on a short "strip club" scene in the film. In the interview Lamb expresses that it took place after "their car blows up," but when I was scanning through the scrips I was able to get my hands on, I suspect it might have been what was denoted the roadhouse scene earlier that same night (before the car fire) and shared in the chapter "A Little Trouble on the Home Front" where Neal is on the phone. The script describes the background to Neal's phone call with "we see a stage with a GIRL dancing behind a shower curtain. A packed house cheers her on." The scene involved a lot of improv and fun banter between Lamb's character and John Candy. Lamb didn't learn the scene had been cut until watching the film at a cast and crew screening. She was devastated, because it had been the first "big thing" that she had done at that time.

- The green convertible that Del rented is a 1986 Chrysler LeBaron Town and Country, with a 2.2-liter turbo engine. It was modified for the film, including the following Dodge 600 parts: taillights, steering wheel, and owner's manual which can be seen in the glove compartment when Neil puts his wallet in there. The trunk was from an older K-car convertible with no third brake light. The luggage rack that appears was not offered in 1986 but was on older models.

- The exterior of the rental car was designed to resemble that of the Griswold's' station wagon, from John Hughes' 1983 film *National Lampoon's Vacation*.

- The license plate on the rental car is a Missouri plate and reads D5N 378.

- There is an entire section of the final shooting script that has numerous electrical functions, including a robotic voice that repeatedly states things like: "THE TRUNK LID IS AJAR. PLEASE SECURE IT BEFORE PROCEEDING." This joke with the computer voice, of course, occurs again in the scene immediately after Del and Neal scrape between the two transport trucks while driving the wrong way, and the trunk lid and Del's steamer trunk go sailing through the air.

- Many of the film's highway scenes were filmed on a stretch of U.S. Highway 219 that runs between Buffalo and Springville, New York, and which had been unopened at the time.

- The highway night scenes were filmed in central California. In order to make the roads appear as if they were in the Midwest in winter, fake snow was applied to the sides of the highways and roads.

- Del is grooving to the song "Mess Around" by Ray Charles while Neal sleeps in the seat beside him. Both Ray Charles and John Candy had starring roles in the 1980 film *The Blues Brothers*. Candy played a police detective while Charles played a music store owner.

- As Del and Neal are pulling in to the El Rancho hotel in their burned-out car, Del says: "You could've killed me, slugging me in the gut when I wasn't ready. That's how Houdini died you know?" What he says is partially true. Harry Houdini had boasted he could withstand hard punches to the stomach. During an incident involving a student at McGill University, Houdini was punched repeatedly in the stomach. Though the magician suffered tremendous pain, the punch itself isn't what killed him. But it did lead to his death. Everyone thought the pain he experienced over the following day or so was from the punch, but it was actually peritonitis from a ruptured appendix. This condition was undiscovered because of the stomach pain from the student's attack and was untreated until it was too late. I wrote about that incident in detail in my co-authored 2018 Dundurn book *Macabre Montreal*.

- The El Rancho Hotel is located on U.S. Highway 41 in Gurnee, Illinois, however, it now operates under a different name.

- Del and Neal stay in room 6 of the El Rancho Hotel.

- The Casio watch that Del tries, unsuccessfully to bribe the hotel clerk with is a model A159W. At the time of the writing of this book, that model is still in production and is still available for purchase.

- In the motel room Steve Martin rents at the El Rancho Motel, there is an amateur painting of Roy Orbison on the wall between the beds.

- When Del and Neal are drinking in their hotel room Del says he's going to Jamaica and says a few lines in a Jamaican accent. A few years later Candy played the manager of the Jamaican bobsled team in 1993's *Cool Runnings*.

- When Del jokes, "I feel like a Whopper. Turn me over, I'm done on this side" he is partially quoting St. Lawrence, a deacon and martyr who lived in Rome. St. Lawrence made the same joke as he was being martyred by being roasted alive on a grill. Among other things, St. Lawrence is now known as the patron saint of comedians.

- Del and Neal are pulled over by a Wisconsin State Trooper played by Michael McKean. Though McKean is only in one scene and is on-screen for perhaps ninety seconds in total, he received fourth billing. McKean's role was initially meant to be much longer. In that original sequence of events, during a longer conversation the State Trooper informs them they overshot Chicago a hundred or so miles back, noting they were driving north, and were actually now in Wisconsin. Upon hearing this news, and realizing he could have been home by then, Neal attacks Del and chases him around the car, which the trooper breaks up.

- Driving from St. Louis to Chicago through Wisconsin would be extremely out of the way, which could explain the added time shown for travel, as driving from St. Louis to Chicago would only take about five hours. It also would explain why the truck they are riding in approaches downtown Chicago from the northwest.

- John Candy uses the same line in two movies: "I know it's not pretty to look at, but it'll get you where you wanna go." He says that about the car to the police officer. He also says it in *Cool Runnings* (1993) when revealing the team's bobsled for the first time.

- Actor Troy Evans, later known for his roles in such television programs as *ER* (Frank Martin) and *Bosch* (Detective "Barrel" Johnson) appeared in an uncredited role in the film as the shy/nervous truck driver. His part was initially supposed to be about one day's work for a nominal fee. Bad weather conditions forced a circumstance where Evans was required to stay for several days and resulted in him earning enough to have apparently made a down payment on a house.

- Within a few shots in the scenes involving the truck driven by Troy Evans, the anti-social truck driver, as well as a few other scenes towards the end of the film Del can be seen with a black eye. This is a reference to a deleted scene where, after Del and Neal are arrested by the state trooper and they leave the jailhouse, Del mentions not having bought insurance for the rental car they destroyed. As a result, Neal punches him in the face.

- The film's plot went through several revisions during production, including the ending. As originally conceived, Del boards the Chicago commuter train with Neal and follows him all the way home. During the editing process, Hughes decided to change the ending so that Del would "take the hint" and allow Neal to return home alone. But in order to get the new ending, Hughes and editor Paul Hirsch had to locate footage of Steve Martin on the Chicago train from a previously deleted scene. All this footage had been shot without Martin ever realizing the camera was on. His laughter and facial expressions perfectly matched what Hughes had been looking for in the flashback scenes with Del. Hughes remarked that Martin had a "beautiful expression" in those unguarded and unscripted moments.

- Within the original intended ending sequences, when Del confesses to Neal that his wife Marie has been dead for eight years, he reveals what he is carrying around in that massive trunk: the remnants of Del's domestic life with Marie. These remnants are described as: "A lamp, some sheets, towels, pictures, a couple pans, fragile things wrapped in newspaper." After he opens the trunk to show Neal, he explains it. "I didn't have much family," he says. "Once she was gone, I sold the house. I didn't feel much like being there. My life was empty enough as it was. I couldn't handle the thought of rambling around the place without Marie there, so I closed it up, took a few things and I've been on the road ever since."

- Many viewers of the film have remarked that the house used as Neal's family home is the same as the one used in the 1990 Hughes film *Home Alone*. If you look closely, you'll see a few details that help absolve this myth. One of them is the "T" shaped intersection of the Page home. The house that was used as Neal's family home is actually in Kenilworth, Illinois, on Warwick. According to a 2012 article on *Hooked on Houses*, the more than 3500 square foot house, which has 6 bedrooms and 4 baths, was built in 1916. The house was listed, in 2012, for approximately $1.8 million. Seven interior sets were built for filming in that house, which took 5 months and cost $100,000. This apparently caused turmoil on the set and angered Paramount executives. The house used in *Home Alone* was on Lincoln Avenue in Winnetka, one town over.

- The movie ends touchingly with a close-up freeze frame of John Candy's tight-lipped grin. *Uncle Buck* (1989) ends the same way, with a frozen frame image of Candy offering the same expression.

- The final script for the film has it ending with the family sitting around the dinner table. Del expresses that he's always had a lot to be thankful for, but "never more than right now." Neal replies: "Same here, pal." Young Marti then begins to recite the Pilgrim Toast for Thanksgiving, with a little help from Susan and Del. Everyone then joins in, and the last line is Del saying: "Amen." As written, that scene is a little reminiscent of Tiny Tim's line of "God bless us, everyone!" in *A Christmas Carol*. (And doesn't Neal's character go through a similar growth that Scrooge does in that Dicken's classic?)

- At the end of the credits, there is a short scene showing Neal's boss is still at his desk in the New York office, analyzing the ads. The man's Thanksgiving dinner sits nearby on his desk. At least Neal made it home.

- That type of "post-credit" scene was something Hughes had done before. He did it in *Ferris Bueller's Day Off* with the title character coming out and telling the audience that it's over and to go home. Ryan Reynolds spoofed this at the end of *Deadpool*, wearing a similar housecoat to the one Matthew Broderick wore and mimicking that moment.

YOU'RE F*CKED!
The car rental f-bomb scene

One of most memorable and quoted moments is when Neal returns to the car rental counter at the St. Louis airport.

That scene is exactly one minute long from the time Neal starts his tirade to the clerk's final retort. In those sixty seconds, the "F" word is used nineteen times (eighteen by Page). If it weren't for this single scene, the film would've easily been rated PG or PG-13 by the MPAA.

Edie McClurg, the woman who plays the rental car agent, was also in the John Hughes film *Ferris Bueller's Day Off* (1986). Edie was approached by John Hughes who gave her a page of script featuring the car rental scene and asked her to read both parts out loud. McClurg believed he was just checking some script to see how it turned out. When she finished, Hughes didn't say anything, and they went about their regular business. A few months later she received a call from Hughes in which he offered her the part of the rental agent.

As was standard for the director, he requested that Edie McClurg partially improvise parts of that scene. Hughes told her to simply pretend to be finishing off a telephone conversation while Neal Page silently fumes as he waits for her to finish.

The take that was used in the film came after Hughes suggested that McClurg ad lib the conversation as if it were a personal one, talking about Thanksgiving plans. On the spot she came up with the idea to speak with her sister about who was going to make what for the family dinner. McClurg apparently drew inspiration from her own life for that pretend dialogue she was having.

In an interview McClurg claimed that to this day random people who recognize her approach her and ask her to tell them they're fucked.

Steve Martin was convinced to join the production after favoring two scenes he had read from the script: the seat adjustment-scene, and the F-word tirade.

In a May 28, 2021, appearance on *Jimmy Kimmel Live!* Actress Emma stone, a huge fan of the film, recited that rant.

Here's the rant from the final film.

You can start by wiping that fucking dumb ass smile off your rosy fucking cheeks! Then you can give me a fucking automobile! A fucking Datsun, a fucking Toyota, a fucking Mustang, a fucking Buick! Four fucking wheels and a seat!

And I really don't care for the way your company left me in the middle of fucking nowhere with fucking keys to a fucking car that isn't fucking there. And I really didn't care to fucking walk down a fucking highway and across a fucking runway to get back here to have you smile at my fucking face.

I want a fucking car, right fucking now.

Here is that scene as it appeared in the "final shooting script" from June 1987.

INT. AIRPORT. ELECTRIC DOORS. NIGHT

The doors open and Neal shuffles in. We start on his expensive Italian shoes and MOVE UP. The shoes are soaked with water, stained with road salt, frayed and torn, a tassel is loose and dragging. We move up to his pant legs. The cuff on one leg is ripped and trailing behind, the fabric is soaked with water and stained with salt and mud. His beautiful trousers are flacked with mud and salt. His overcoat is splattered with water and dirt. He stops as WE LAND ON HIS FACE. It's frozen and speckled with the same salt and grit. His eyes are wild with rage, his teeth are clenched, his hair is standing on end and glistening with frost. He's wrapped his necktie around his head to keep his ears warm. He looks left, then right. His upper lip pulls back and he snarls.

INT. AIRPORT. RENTAL CAR COUNTER. NIGHT

A perky, young GIRL is happily tapping on the keys of her computer. She looks up with a big, friendly TV commercial smile. A beat and the smile dissolves.

HER POV

Neal stands before her, crazed, frozen and mad as hell.

CU. GIRL

She manages to put on another giant smile.

> GIRL
> May I help you?

CU. NEAL

He leans forward. Talks very softly.

> NEAL
> Yes.

CU GIRL

She leans forward to hear better.

> GIRL
> (softly)
> How many I help you?

INT. CAR RENTAL COUNTER

He leans a little closer. She leans a little closer.

> NEAL
> You can start by wiping that fuckin' dumb-
> ass smile off your rosy fuckin' cheeks.

CU. GIRL

She's stunned.

INT. RENTAL CAR COUNTER.

Neal continues his tirade.

> NEAL
> Then you can drop the Miss Fuckin'
> Cheerful bullcrap and give me a fuckin'
> automobile. A fuckin' Mustang, a fuckin'
> Toyota, a fuckin' Datsun, a fuckin' Chevy,
> four fuckin' wheels and a <u>seat</u>!

The girl regains her composure, clears her throat,
fidgets with her uniform scarf.

> GIRL

I don't really care for the way you're talking
to me

NEAL

I don't really care for the way your fuckin'
company left me out in the middle of
fuckin' nowhere with fuckin' keys to a
fuckin' car that isn't fuckin' there. And I
didn't really care to fuckin' walk down a
fuckin' runway to get back here to have you
smile in my fuckin' face. I'm a pretty
fuckin' nice guy under normal
circumstances and I have nothing against
you except your fuckin' happy demeanor
too violently illustrates to me how miserable
I am. I want a fuckin' car, right fuckin'
<u>now</u>!

GIRL

Do you still have your rental agreement?

NEAL

No.

The girl clicks her tongue.

GIRL

Oh, boy.

NEAL

Oh, boy, what?

GIRL

You're fucked.

THE MUSIC
A look at the Soundtrack

It has been said that music is one of the most powerful ways to establish emotion or to set the scene. Movies have been leveraging powerful scores and soundtracks to that end for years. And *Planes, Trains and Automobiles* is no exception.

In the February 2021 *John Hughes: 5 Movie Collection* Blu-Ray special feature called "Heartbreak and Triumph: The Legacy of John Hughes" several people who worked closely with John Hughes commented on just how central music was to his work and his life.

Songs such as "Pretty in Pink" by the Psychedelic Furs, could inspire an entire movie. Or even a band like Simple Minds could write music that captured the essence of what the teenagers experience in a film like *The Breakfast Club*. Can you ever hear the song "Don't You (Forget About Me) without thinking about that scene with Judd Nelson walking across an empty football field and thrusting a hand triumphantly in the air?

The soundtrack for *Planes, Trains and Automobiles* leverages an eclectic and effective mix of rock, pop, and country music. Released in 1987 on CD and in vinyl formats, it has since gone out of print. A digital version of the album is available on iTunes/Apple Music as of the writing of this in August 2021.

Who can forget the brilliant track of the Emmlou Harris version of "Back in Baby's Arms" playing when Neal and Del wake up to discover they have been cuddling with each other in their sleep? The dialogue and choreography of that scene when they wake up is a cinematic classic moment, particularly when Neal asks Del where his one hand is, and he replies that it's between two pillows. The shout of "Those Aren't pillows!" followed by the two men leaping out of bed then starting to talk in stereotypical "masculine" script mentioning sports is not how it appears in a 2/6/87 version of the script.

INT. BEDROOM. CU. DEL AND NEAL.
MORNING.

Sleeping. Tight as spoons. Del has his arm around
Neal's chest. Neal's holding Del's hand. Del's face
is in the crook of Neal's neck. Nestled tight and
warm. They're both sleeping, sweet and satisfied.
Del snuggles and nibbles Neal's earlobe with his
dry lips. Neal smiles in his sleep. A beat and the
smile relaxes. Somewhere in his unconscious mind,
he senses something's not right. Another beat and
Neal opens his eyes. He thinks for a moment. He
slowly brings Del's hand up to his face and looks
at it. Del's eyes open. He looks around, orients
himself. He knows something's terribly wrong.

                          DEL
    Neal?

                          NEAL
    Del?

                          DEL
    Why are you holding my hand?

                          NEAL
    Why did you kiss my ear?

                          DEL
    I don't know.

                          NEAL
    Where's your other hand?

                        DEL
                      (worried)
        I'm not sure.

                        NEAL
        Find it, Del!

Del thinks another beat. His hand emerges from
under Neal's pillow.

                        NEAL
        On the count of three. One…

                        DEL
        Two…

                    NEAL AND DEL
        THREE!

INT. ROOM. MORNING.

Del and Neal burst out of the bed, screaming and
shivering with revulsion.

   Sadly, there are songs used in the movie
that do not appear on the soundtrack. The
missing songs include "Mess Around" by
Ray Charles (which Del lip syncs and air
plays while driving as Neal sleeps in the
passenger seat beside him), "Blue Moon
of Kentucky" by Bill Monroe (Neal and

Del sing along to it playing on the radio in the fire-damaged rental car), and "Everytime You Go Away" performed by Blue Room (a cover of the Paul Young song that plays during the final homecoming scene in the film.)

Here are some other interesting behind-the-scenes details about the music that fans are likely to find interesting.

That Rockin' Valley

The score, by Ira Neborn, which has been described as frenetic, makes solid use of a rock and roll adaptation of a classic folk and country song. "Red River Rock," performed by a new wave virtual British Band called Silicon Teens is an electronic version of the more rock styled version released by Johnny and the Hurricanes.

The original "Red River Valley" was written by Jules Verne Allen sometime around 1890 and has long been re-adapted by different regions where it was performed and sung with the "Red River" being replaced by other locales such as

"Bright Little" or "Bright Laurel." The first commonly known recording of the song was the 1925 version under the name "Cowboy Love Song" by Texas musician Carl T. Sprague who was sometimes referred to as "The Original Singing Cowboy."

According to an entry in the 1973 book *The Penguin Book of Canadian Folks Songs* by Edith Fowke and Keith MacMillan, anecdotal evidence exists that the song may have originally been composed in Canada during the 1870 Wolseley Expedition to the Red River Valley in Manitoba. In the version of the lyrics that Fowke uncovered, the song recounts a Métis girl lamenting the departure of her Anglo lover, a soldier who arrived in the west during the Red River Rebellion of 1870.

Every Time Elton John Goes Away

Elton John and Gary Osborne were originally commissioned to write and perform the theme song for *Planes, Trains and Automobiles*. They were almost finished writing it and were scheduled to record a few days later when Paramount Pictures issued an unexpected demand that this original song master become property of the studio.

Elton was under contractual obligation with Polygram that he would sign all rights to his released music to them. Since Polygram wouldn't allow it, Elton was not able to continue. Both Elton John and Gary Osborne had to withdraw from the project because Paramount and Polygram could not come to an agreement. The song they had been working on was never recorded.

John Hughes wanted Paramount to license Paul Young's 1985 number one hit cover version of the Hall & Oates 1980 song "Everytime You Go Away" as the movie's theme song. Despite Young approving of the song's use for the film, his record company denied the request.

Paramount opted to use a cover version of the song by Blue Room (featuring vocals by Linda Hall), which was never released. Versions of the song including cuts from the movie end credits, have been released to places like YouTube.

The song that eventually became known as the "unofficial" theme of the movie is an instrumental version of "Power to Believe" by The Dream Academy. The band performed this version at the request of John Hughes, and it is considered to be Del Griffith's unofficial theme song. That special instrumental version doesn't appear on the official 1987 soundtrack and wasn't released until The Dream Academy included it in their 2014 compilation album *The Morning Lasted All Day: A Retrospective.*

Six Days on The Road and Many Years on the Charts

A 1987 Steve Earle & The Dukes recording of the song "Six Days on the Road" was used in the scene where Del continues to fiddle with the car seat adjustment in the passenger seat of the rental car.

The song, which was recognized as a celebration of the American truck driver and kicked off a trend of similar songs about truck drivers and the working man, was written by Earl Green and Carl Mongomery. It was initially recorded by Paul Davis in 1961. Dave Dudley recorded it again in 1963, where it became a hit, reaching #2 on the *Billboard* Hot Country Songs chart. The song remained on the charts for twenty-one weeks.

Numerous artists have recorded the song over the years, including Johnny Rivers, Charley Pride, Boxcar Willie, George Jones, Jim Croce, George Thorogood, and Wolfman Jack.

Sawyer Brown's 1997 version of the song, which made it to #13 featured altered lyrics, with the "I'm taking little white pills" (a reference to stimulant drug use) to "I'm passing little white lines."

The version recorded by Steve Earle in 1987 for *Planes, Trains and Automobiles* hit #29 on the *Billboard* Hot Country Singles chart in 1988.

Soundtrack Credits

Ba-Na-Na-Bam-Boo (1987)
Written by Elizabeth Westwood, Nick Burton, and Robert Andrews
Performed by Westworld
Produced by Mark Ferda
Westworld performs courtesy of BMG Records Ltd.

Back in Baby's Arms (1963)
Written by Bob Montgomery
Performed by Emmylou Harris
Produced by Jimmy Bowen & Emmylou Harris
Emmylou Harris performs courtesy of Warner Bros. Records Inc.

Blue Moon of Kentucky (1948)
Written by Bill Monroe
Performed by Steve Martin (uncredited) & John Candy (uncredited)

Continental Trailways Blues (1987)
Written by Steve Earle
Performed by Steve Earle and John Mandoukos (as The Dukes)
Produced by Steve Earle and Tony Brown
Steve Earle performs courtesy of MCA Records

Everytime You Go Away (1980)
Written by Daryl Hall
Performed by Blue Room
Produced by Steve Levine

Lost Again (1983)
Written by Boris Blank & Dieter Meier

Performed and produced by Yello
Courtesy of Polygram Special Products, a division of Polygram Records, Inc.

I'll Show You Something Special (1987)
Written by Des Morris, Mark Morris, and Steve Brown
Performed by Baalam & the Angel
Produced by Steve Brown
Baalam & the Angel performs courtesy of Virgin Records Ltd.

Mess Around (1953)
Written by Ahmet Ertegun
Performed by Ray Charles
Produced by Ahmet Ertegun & Jerry Wexler
Courtesy of Atlantic Recording Corp., a division of Warner Special Products

(Meet) the Flintstones (1961)
Music by Hoyt Curtin (as Hoyt S. Curtin)
Lyrics by William Hanna and Joseph Barbera
Performed by John Candy (uncredited)

Modigliani (Lost in Your Eyes) (1985)
Written by Susan Ottaviano, Jade Lee, and Theodore Ottaviano
Performed by Book of Love
Produced by Ivan Ivan
Courtesy of Sire Records
By Arrangement with Warner Special Products
Power to Believe (1987)
Written by Nick Laird-Clowes and Gilbert Gabriel
Performed by The Dream Academy
Produced by Hugh Padgham and Nick Laird-Clowes
Courtesy of Reprise Records
By Arrangement with Warner Special Products

Red River Rock (1959)
Written by Tom King, Ira Mack, and Fred Mendelsohn
Performed by Silicon Teens

Six Days on the Road (1959)
Written by Earl Green and Carl B. Montgomery
Performed by Steve Earle and John Mandoukos (as The Dukes)
Produced by Steve Earle and Tony Brown
Steve Earle performs courtesy of MCA Records

Three Coins in the Fountain (1954)
Music by Jule Styne
Lyrics by Sammy Cahn
Performed by Steve Martin (uncredited)

Wheels (1969)
Written by Chris Hillman & Gram Parsons (as Graham Parsons)
Performed by Stars of Heaven
Produced by Paul Barrett

I Can Take Anything (1987)
(Love theme from Planes, Trains & Automobiles (1987))
Written by David Steele, Andy Cox, and John Hughes
Performed by E.T.A. featuring Steve Martin and John Candy

Gonna Move (1987)
Written by Dave Edmunds & Nick Lowe
Performed and Produced by Dave Edmunds

DEL-ISMS
From the film & the cutting-room floor

Del Griffith has a lot of unique (no, that's not Latin for "asshole") sayings in the movie that are cheeky, hilarious sayings or memorable quotes.

Del's character, who is a combination of brilliant writing by Hughes and phenomenal acting by Candy, has inspired countless other creators. Including me.

I loosely based some of the traits (including the frank humor and verbal diarrhea ramblings) of a recurring character in my *Canadian Werewolf* series, on Del. Buddy J. Samuels, my main character's traveling salesman friend, is a subtle nod to Candy's portrayal of Del Griffith.

Following are a collection of some Del-isms as brilliantly delivered by John Candy in the film.

[During their first face to face encounter at the airport in New York.]

Del: I know you, don't I? I'm usually very good with names but I'll be damned if I haven't forgotten yours.

Neal: You stole my cab.

Del: I never stole anything in my life.

Neal: I hailed a cab on Park Avenue this afternoon and before I could get in it you stole it.

Del: You're the guy who tried to get my cab. I knew I knew you! You scared the bejesus out of me. Come to think of it, it was easy to get a cab during rush hour.

[While sitting together on the flight from New York to Chicago.]

Neal: Look, I don't want to be rude, but I'm not much of a conversationalist, and I really want to finish this article, a friend of mine wrote it, so...

Del: Don't let me stand in your way, please don't let me stand in your way. The last thing I want to be remembered as is an annoying blabbermouth. You know, nothing grinds my gears worse than some chowderhead that doesn't know when to keep his big trap shut. If you catch me running off with my mouth, just give me a poke on the chubs.

[*During New York to Chicago flight.*]

Del: Six bucks and my right nut says we're not landing in Chicago.

[*Shortly after landing in Wichita on their re-routed flight.*]

Del: You know, the finest line a man will walk is between success at work and success at home. I gotta motto: Like your work, Love your wife.

[*At Wichita airport.*]

Neal: What's the flight situation?
Del: Simple. There's no way on earth we're going to get out of here tonight. We'd have more luck playing pickup sticks with our butt-cheeks than we will getting a flight out of here before daybreak.
Neal: I guess we'll find out soon enough.
Del: Yeah, but by the time the airline cancels this flight, which they will sooner or later, you'd have more of a chance to find a three-legged ballerina than you would a hotel room.

[*In the lobby at the Braidwood Motel in Wichita.*]

Gus: Del Griffith! How the hell are ya?

Del: Well, I'm still a million bucks shy of bein' a millionaire.

[*After Neal's angry and hurtful rant about how Del blathers on too much and doesn't know when to shut up.*]

Del: You wanna hurt me? Go right ahead if it makes you feel any better. I'm an easy target. Yeah, you're right, I talk too much. I also listen too much. I could be a cold-hearted cynic like you... but I don't like to hurt people's feelings. Well, you think what you want about me; I'm not changing. I like... I like me. My wife likes me. My customers like me. 'Cause I'm the real article. What you see is what you get.

[*At breakfast in Wichita when Neal mentions the airline said he had a good chance of getting on standby.*]

Del: If they told you wolverines would make good house pets, would you believe them?

[At bus station in Jefferson City.]

Del: I guess this is probably a good time as any to tell you this. Our tickets are only good to St. Louis. St. Louis to Chi-town is booked tighter than Tom Thumb's ass.

[To the taxi stand agent at the St. Louis Airport who tells him to get his car out of way.]

Del: What is your problem? You insensitive asshole.

[In rental car after leaving the St. Louis airport.]

Del: I've never seen a guy get picked up by his testicles before. Lucky thing for you that cop passed by when he did. Otherwise, you'd be lifting up your schnutz to tie your shoes. I'm sorry. That's terrible. Do you have any idea how glad I am I didn't kill you?

Neal: *[high voice]* Do you have any idea how glad I'd be if you had?

Del: Oh, come on, pal, you don't mean that. Remember what I said about going with the flow?

Neal: How am I supposed to go with the flow when the rental car agency leaves me in a 100-acre parking lot with keys to a car that isn't there then I have to hike back 3 miles to find out they don't have any more cars?

Del: I got a car, no sweat at all.

Neal: Well, Del, you're a charmed man.

Del: Nope.

Neal: Oh, I know. You just go with the flow.

Del: Like a twig on the shoulders of a mighty stream.

[*As another driver across the divided highway is trying to alert them that they're driving on the wrong side of the highway.*]

Neal: He says we're going the wrong way...

Del: Oh, he's drunk. How would he know where we're going?

[*Speaking to himself while sitting in the car in the snow at a motel where Neal is inside.*]

Del: Well Marie, once again my dear, you were as right as rain. I am, without a doubt, the biggest pain in the butt that ever came down the pike. I meet someone whose company I really enjoy, and what do I do? I go overboard. I smother the poor soul. I cause him more trouble than he has a right to. God, I got a big mouth. When am I ever gonna wake up? I wish you were here with me right now. But...I guess that's not gonna happen. Not now, anyway.

[In motel room after a few drinks of the night where they drove in the car it had caught on fire.]

Del: Was that seat hot or what? I feel like a Whopper. Turn me over, I'm done on this side. I'm afraid to look at my ass. There'll be griddle marks.

[In motel room after drinking and laughing together.]

Neal: Let me close this conversation by saying that you are one unique individual.
Del: Unique... what's that, Latin for "asshole"?

[In motel room after Neal mentions that at the very least, Del has woman he loves to grow old with.]

Neal: You love her, don't you?

Del: Love...is not a big enough word. It's not a big enough word for how I feel about my wife.

Del-isms From the Script

There were many other Del-isms in the final version of the script that didn't make it into the film. Or ones that were used in the script within longer scenes that didn't fully make the cut.

Below are Del-isms as they appear in the original script. (*Please note that I tried to preserve the original script, typos, and all*)

[*While waiting in New York at the airport for the delayed flight, Neal encounters Del in the men's room.* (NOT IN FILM)]

INT. MEN'S ROOM. NIGHT.

Neal walks in. We HEAR LOUD WHISTLING. Neal stops and looks.

HIS POV

Del's in his undershirt, face lathered, razor in hand, dop kit opened on the sink. He looks around and sees Neal. He smiles.

                        DEL
                  Howdy traveller!

NEAL

Returns a lame smile and crosses to the urinal.

DEL

He continues shaving

                        DEL
          On the road quite a bit? I am. I know these
          airlines like the back of my hand. An hour
          delay means an hour and a half. Your nickel
          against my nuts it's snowing in Chi-town.
          It's the damn lake. All that…moisture.
          Chicago goes and the whole national air
          transportation system takes a dump. If you
          told me it was raining rabbit pellets in
          Chicago, I'd believe you. And weather
          town. Great pizza, the best hot dogs in the
          world, great parks. Damn nice zoo. Good
          aquarium, excellent art museum, although
          I've never been there personally.
          Knowledgeable cab drivers. Good
          newspapers. Nice hotels. A bit high priced
          but comfortable. You enjoy blues music?
          Blues? You like the blues?

He turns.

HIS POV

Neal's gone.

[*During their first conversation on the plane shortly after introducing them-selves to one another.* (PARTS APPEAR IN FILM)]

                    DEL
What's your business, Neal Page?

                    NEAL
Marketing.

                    DEL
Marketing? Super! I love marketing. I do a little of that game myself.

He reaches under the seat, pops his briefcase open and pulls out a calendar. He flips it open and shows it to Neal.

CU. CALENDAR

A busty, naked girl in a shower holding curtain rings.

DEL AND NEAL

Neal winces at the unpleasant photo. Del flips the calendar closed and offers it to Neal.

                    DEL
This was my idea. Keep it.

                    NEAL
No, thanks.

> DEL
>
> Go ahead. I have plenty.

Neal shakes his head.

> DEL
>
> Take it for Pete's sake.

Neal takes the calendar.

> DEL
>
> If you've got a shower curtain in your home, there's a fifty/fifty chance that the rings holding it up were sold to your supplier by me. I like to kid that if it weren't for shower curtain rings, Janet Leigh probably wouldn't have caught her lunch in "Psycho." You see that flick?

Neal nods yes.

> DEL
>
> I like to joke but that one was no joke. I was new to the business when that baby hit the silver screen and that shower murder left a crap stain on the reputation of shower curtains the size of Texas. Pebble glass shower doors took a big bite out of our sales for several years. We're back on our feet now. We're doing good. The young people going into their first homes don't have the same phobia about showers that their parents had. That Alfred Hitchcock. You know what that "Birds" film did to parakeet [sales]? El Dumpo, Jack. Sewer City. Good

friend of mine lost his shirt. You use
curtains or doors in your home?

Neal stares at him.

DEL
Doors? Hell, it's no sweat off my back. I'm
just happy to have someone to talk to. I finished my book about an hour ago. Filthy
goddarn thing. When you travel as much as
I do, you run out of reading material. If it's
been published, I've read it. Fiction, non-
fiction, the classics – Robbins, Krantz,
Iacocca. You name it, I've read it. I got so
hard-up last week on a layover in Atlanta, I
read a biography of Prince. That's not his
real name, by the way, It's Rogers Nelson.

Neal smiles politely.

NEAL
I don't want to be rude but I really have [a
lot] of work to do.

Neal stares at him.

DEL
Don't let me stand in your way. The last
thing I want to be remembered as is an annoying blabbermouth. Nothing grinds my
gears worse than some chowderhead who
doesn't know when to keep his big trap
shut. They've got "no smoking" signs; they
oughta have "no talking" signs. There've
been plenty of times when I would have
switched that sucker on, believe you me. If

you catch me running off at the mouth, give
me a good poke in the nose.

Del reaches into the seat pocket in front of him and
removes the airline magazine. Neal bends over and
opens his crushed briefcase. He takes out a bound
report. Del glances down at the briefcase.

DEL
What the heck happened to your briefcase?
Looks like a vehicle ran over it.

NEAL
Cab.

DEL
What a shame! What'd you pay for
it?

Neal is reluctant to answer. It's none of Del's
business.

DEL
Gift? Mine, too. Gift from the company for
getting the shower ring contract for the U.S.
Navy. You know how many rings that baby
was worth?

NEAL
I have no idea.

DEL
Try 37 million.

Neal smiles and opens his report.

DEL
I figure that over the next years several
millions of sailors are going to use those
showers with our rings and if they take the
time to inquire about the rings and they feel
they're good rings, when they get out of the
service and consider shower rings they'll
select ours.

NEAL
Can you excuse me?

DEL
Sorry. I'm being a blabbermouth, aren't I?

Neal sighs. Del's driving him mad.

NEAL
I really have to finish…

Del holds up his hand, cutting Neal off. He leans
back in his seat and opens the magazine. Neal
opens his report. They both read for a few moments.

DEL
You know why we're not taking off? Bet
you three bucks and my left nut Chicago's
socked in.

[*Later on the flight.* (ONLY THE DEL-ISM, DELIVERED IN A SLIGHTLY AL-TERED FASHION, MADE IT INTO THE FILM)]

INT. PLANE. WIDE. LATER

The lights are out except for the occasional reading lamp.

INT. PLANE. NEAL.

Neal's sipping a coffee, going over his water-stained papers. He sets down the reports and looks at his watch. He glances at Del.

HIS POV

Del's facing him, just inches away, eyes closed, mouth open, toothpick dangling from his lips, snoring like a sow. His calculator watch alarm is BEEPING.

CU. NEAL.

Staring at Del.

HIS POV

Del opens his eyes.

> DEL
> Six bucks and my right nut we're not
> landing in Chicago.

He shuts off his watch alarm and goes back to
sleep.

[*At the airport in Witchita after Neal gets
off the phone with his wife.* (AN AL-
TERED VERSION OF THIS SCENE
WAS CUT FOR THE FILM)]

DEL
A little trouble on the home front?

As far as Neal's concerned, his home life is none of
Del's business.

DEL
Sounded like things were getting a little
testy.

NEAL
I don't think that's any of your concern.

DEL
Probably not. I thought you might want to
air some feelings.

NEAL
I don't.

DEL
The finest line a man'll ever walk is
between success at work and success at
home. You know what my motto is? Love
your wife, like your work.

A polite pause. Neal isn't accepting advice from Del.

NEAL
I'll remember that. What's the flight situation?

DEL
Simple. There's no way on Earth we're talking off from here tonight. We'd have more luck playing pick-up-sticks with our butt cheeks than getting out of here before daybreak.

NEAL
There are other airlines.

DEL
One goes belly-up, the others are sure to follow. I may not know the price of Eggs in Sweden, but I know the U.S. air transport system and when you waylay to Witchita enroute to Chicago, you're up the creek. I'd venture to say Old Man Winter's busting records in Chicago right now.

Neal's a little worried that Del may be right. But he's not prepared to take any advice.

NEAL
I guess I'll find out soon enough.

DEL
By the time you wait for the airlines to pull the plug on the flight, which they will

sooner or later, you'll have an easier time
finding a three-legged ballerina than a hotel
room. I know Witchita. I know airlines. I
know the hotel scene. They start diverting
flights here and you don't book a room,
you're looking at a couple nights on a dirty
floor.

NEAL
You're saying I'll be stuck in Witchita?

DEL
I'm saying you <u>are</u> stuck in Witchita.

[*There are a few Gus-isms in the script
that also didn't make the cut. Gus is the
owner of the Braidwood Inn, which, in the
script is called the Interstate Inn. This is
from the lobby of that hotel.*]

INT. LOBBY. NIGHT

Fake wood and [naugahyde]. A tiny front desk, two
sofas, a rack of tourist info, a pay phone, a
newspaper box and an easel with a cardboard sign
with words in glitter – LISA PELSTRAM'S
ACCORDIAN REVUE. Del and Neal lug the trunk
into the lobby and set it down.

DEL
Evening Gus.

The DESK CLERK stands up from his chair where he's sitting watching TV.

                    GUS
    Del Griffith? How the hell are you?

                    DEL
    I'm still a million bucks shy of being a
    millionaire. How are you?

                    GUS
    I was doing pretty good there for a while but
    Sunday I pissed my pants during 60
    Minutes so I guess I gotta go back in for
    more plumbing work.

                    DEL
    Tough break, Gus. I'd like you to meet an
    old friend of mine. This is Neal Page. Neal,
    this is Gus Mooney.

Gus reaches his hand across the desk. Neal shakes
it.

                    NEAL
    Glad to meet you.

                    GUS
    Likewise.

                    DEL
    We were flying into Chicago from New
    York and a storm brought us here.

GUS

I know all about it. I must got half your
flight already booked in. Now tell me, Del,
am I just getting old or are they letting fat
gals be stewardesses these days?

DEL

Times change, Gus. I told Neal you'd be
able to fix him up.

Gus clucks his tongue.

GUS

You know, Del, I'd rather shoot arrows out
my ass than disappoint you or a friend of
yours but I'm booked solid. I got three of
those fat girls sharing a single as it is. One
twin and two cots and them cots are really
built for youngsters.

Neal looks at Del with a sigh.

DEL

Nothing, Gus?

GUS

If old Herbert Hoover come back from the
dead and needed a room for the night, I
couldn't help him. Sorry.

[A truly memorable moment is when Neal explodes in rage out of the bed at the Braidwood Inn and rants about Del's freeloading and boring chatter. Interestingly, the long rant about Del's not-stop annoying anecdotes doesn't appear in the script. Also, Del isn't clearing his sinuses, with a final "shave and a haircut" finish that sends Neal into his tirade. Instead, it's the clearing of his throat, followed by the announcement he has to fart.]

Neal turns off the light. He settles back into the bed. There's another long pause. Del clears his throat. Loud and graphic. He repeats it.

> NEAL

What're you doing?

> DEL

Clearing my pipes.

> NEAL

Why?

> DEL

I'm doing it for you.

> NEAL

Don't bother.

> DEL

You like loud snoring?

> NEAL

No.

> DEL

Then let me clear my pipes.

Del snorts a couple more times. The room falls silent for another long beat.

> DEL

Neal?

> NEAL

<u>What!</u>

There's a long pause.

> DEL

I have got to fart something fierce.

Neal rips the covers off and jumps out of bed. He turns on the light. He grabs his pants and slips them on.

> DEL

Hey! I'm just being honest, for Christ's sake! I could have sneaked it on you.

Neal grabs his shirt

> DEL

Where are you going?

> NEAL

I'm sleeping in the lobby.

DEL
Aw, come on! I'll go in the john.

He pulls back the covers and slides his legs over the side of the bed.

DEL
If your kid shits his trousers do you smack him?

Neal stops at the door. He throws a look at Del.

NEAL
What the hell are you talking about?.

DEL
You're not a very tolerant person.

NEAL
I'm a <u>very</u> tolerant person.

DEL
Oh, really?

NEAL
Look, you've been under my skin since New York. You ripped off my cab...

DEL
I know all this. You paid for the room the pizza...you're a tight ass.

NEAL
How'd you like a mouthful of teeth?

DEL

You're hostile, too. Nice personality
combination. Hostile and intolerant. That's
borderline criminal.

NEAL

Screw you! You spill beer all over the bed,
you smoke, you make a mess of the
bathroom…

DEL

And I let you stay in my room. I let you pay
for it so you wouldn't feel like an intruder
which you most certainly are.

NEAL

I'm an intruder?

DEL

You're an intruder. I was having a nice trip
until you walked into my life.

NEAL

I walked into <u>your</u> life? Who talked my ear
off on the plane?

DEL

Who told you to book a room? Out of the
goodness of my dumb old heart, I offered
you help. You're an ungrateful jackass. Go
to sleep in the lobby. Go ahead. I hope you
wake up so stiff you can't move

Neal hesitates at the door.

                    NEAL
You saw me coming. You're no saint. You
get a free room. Free cab. And somebody
who'll listen to your boring stories.

Del glares at Neal.

                    DEL
You want to hurt me? Go ahead. If it makes
you feel better…be my guest. I'm an easy
target. I like people, Neal. I even like you.
People are my business. They're my
business because I've made them my
business. Yeah, I talk too much. I also listen
too much. You can be a cold-hearted cynic.
I don't care. Think what you want about me.
I'm not changing. I like me. My wife likes
me. My customers like me. Because I'm the
real article. I'm a human being. Flaws, fat
and farts. I'm flesh and blood.

CU. NEAL

He feels like the last slice on a loaf of bread.

CU. DEL

He's serious and genuine.

INT. ROOM

Neal closes the door and walks back to the bed. He
steps out of his pants and gets into bed. He turns
out the light. They both settle in.

                    NEAL

Sorry.

                    DEL
(after a long pause)
So am I.

                    NEAL
Night.

                    DEL
Sleep tight.
[pause]
My wife used to say sleep tight, don't let the
bed bugs bite. I've actually never seen a bed
bug. I seen plenty of other things.

Truck lights outside.

                    DEL
    Nah. It's just an old saying.
    (pause)
    Maybe lice.

EXT. MOTEL

A huge semi-tractor pulls up outside the motel
room.

INT. MOTEL

The room is flooded with light.

[At the breakfast diner in Wichita. Part of this scene made it into the film.]

DEL

What'd the airline say?

NEAL

Everything's booked solid but they said I have a good chance of getting on standby.

DEL

Uh, huh. If they told you wolverines make good house pets would you believe them

NEAL

What choice do I have?

DEL

You want to be in Chicago by tonight?

NEAL

At the outside

DEL

Regardless of what the airline told you, and believe me, they'll tell you Abe Lincoln died in a boating accident if they think that it'll prevent a ticket return. Chicago by tonight's a scratch. I think if you plan on tomorrow morning you're still tugging your tamale.

NEAL

I'm not spending Thanksgiving in Wichita. I have a family waiting for me.

DEL
Worse things have happened. Ask any
wartime resident of Dresden.

NEAL
I'm home tonight come hell or high water.

DEL
Which do you prefer? I'm going with the
high water myself. If you think the airline
gives two craps and a doorbell chime if you
eat turkey with your family tomorrow,
you're deluded.

NEAL
I'll get home.

DEL
Not on an airplane. There's 24 hours of air
traffic backed-up. Anyway you slice it, the
odds are you and me are eating turkey right
here.

[*Sitting outside the Braidwood Inn waiting for Gus's son to pick them up and
talking about having been robbed the
night before.*]

DEL
Do you have any checks?

NEAL
My wife keeps the checkbook. You?

                    DEL
Strictly cash. I travel too much to write
checks. 99% of them would be out of state
and an out of state check is about as
welcome as a priest in a whorehouse.

*[At the bus station in Jefferson City. This
cut scene contains a Del-ism that is called
back to later when the two are in the
rental car.]*

Del looks at Neal. Neal's bubbling with anger. He
looks at his watch. Del looks at his.

                    DEL
It's not my fault the train caught on fire.

Neal looks at him. He's not so sure.

                    DEL
Thank your lucky stars it didn't detail. They
derail more often than they catch fire.

                    NEAL
It's three fifteen.

                    DEL
The bus leaves at four. We're alright. Have
you ever thought of going with the flow?

                    NEAL
I am going with the flow and you're what
floated into my life.

[*At the St. Louis bus station restaurant. After the scene where Del has sold a bunch of his shower curtain rings as earings.*]

INT. BUS STATION RESTAURANT. DAY

Del and Neal are eating. Neal is trying to find a way into a chili dog without getting sick to his stomach. His brain says no, his stomach says yes. He closed his eyes and bites. Del has no such trouble.

> DEL
> I'm in the wrong business. You know how many of those damn rings I sold? Dozens. I don't know what got into me but that was a brilliant idea.

Neal takes a slug of beer and washes down the bite of hot dog. He takes another swing and swishes it around his mouth in an attempt to cleanse his palate.

> NEAL
> You didn't have to sell your samples.

> DEL
> I've steered you wrong so many times, I felt like a shit burger on a stale bun. The least I could do was scrape together a nice meal for you.

[Later in the same scene.]

NEAL
I really think we'll both get where we're
going a lot faster on our own.

Del looks down at his plate

DEL
Okay

There's a long pause.

DEL
In other words, I'm a pain in the ass.

NEAL
No, not at all.

DEL
Yeah, I am. Everything I touch turns to shit.
My mother used to tell me I had twice as
much heart as brain.

*[At the St. Louis Airport taxi dispatch
station. Del is standing over Neal, who is
lying on the pavement after having been
punched in the face by the dispatcher.]*

DISPATCHER
Get your car outta there!

DEL
Hey, hold your water, wiseass! We've got
an injured man in the street here. Right
under your damn nose. You get off your fat
duff and help him up. I'll move my car.

[*At night in the rental car. From a cut sce-*
ne that comes after the "you play with
your balls a lot" scene. Neil is driving,
and Del is snoring so loud in the passen-
ger seat it's drowning out the radio. After
doing everything he could possibly think
of to wake Del from an impossible to
wake from sleep, including blasting the
radio and opening all the car windows,
Neal shouts at him]

NEAL
DEL! DEL GRIFFITH! HEY! WAKE UP
STUPID! UP AND AT 'EM LIVER LIPS!

Neal reaches over and pokes Del. He stirs, turns
away and closes his mouth. He stops snoring. Neal
puts the windows back up. He turns off the radio.
Nothing out of Del. He reaches into his lap and
adjusts his crotch

DEL
Just can't leave the walnuts alone, can you?

[Immediately after Del loses control of the car while Neal was sleeping and manages to stop the car after it screams down an exit ramp.]

NEAL
What the hell are you doing?

Del looks at him with eyes wide and wild. Executes a quick recovery.

DEL
You almost had venison in your lap. The biggest deer. I ever saw. At least a ten point buck. Standing in the middle of the highway looking at me like I was a doe in heat.

Neal stares at him.

DEL
If I'd hit it, we'd be human hash. Go back to sleep. We're making good time.

[In the motel lobby after burning up the rental car, as Del is trying to convince the clerk to give him a room without having a credit card and the required $42.]

CLERK
You got $17 and a good watch?

DEL

I've got two bucks and a Casio

                    CLERK
Good night.

The Clerk steps away from the counter.

                    DEL
               (hold up his hat)
I'll throw in my hat. It's a beaut. Warm as
all get out.

The Clerk turns out the lights.

**[*Neal and Del in the motel together after
their rental car caught on fire.*]**

                    NEAL
Hey, I'm sorry I popped you in the gut.

                    DEL
I deserved it.

                    NEAL
No, you didn't.

                    DEL
Sure I did. If I didn't have one foot in my
mouth and the other in a bucket of shit, I
wouldn't recognize myself.

[The next morning when they realize their car is stuck in a huge overnight dumping of snow.]

DEL

We're stuck tighter than two dogs on their wedding night.

[A minute later, as Neal is trying to rock the car to help get it out of the snow.]

DEL

She's starting to grip. A little more. Put your balls into it!

NEAL

I am!

DEL

Squeeze your ass and think of Nazis. We're moving this hunk of shit!

I CAN TAKE ANYTHING!
Mistakes, continuity issues, factual errors, and other minor blunders

Over the years, plenty of observant viewers of the movie have pointed out minor errors, issues, or mistakes that made it into the film.

You can find these, and many more details and commentary on sites like Movie Mistakes (www.moviemistakes.com).

Because I adore the movie, and, chances are, if you're reading this book, you're also a huge fan too, I want to express the fact that pointing out these errors does not, in any way, reduce my love and appreciation of this fantastic film.

Most books that are published, regardless of how many rounds of edits and proofreads, still contain a handful of typos and errors. (So, if you've spotted any in this book, please don't let *that* ruin your enjoyment of this book). Similarly, virtually every film has at least a handful of errors like this.

This chapter includes **Continuity**, **Blooper**, and **Factual** errors that appear in the film.

The accompanying time slots that appear with these are in Hour: Minute: Second using H:MM:SS format and are from a version of the movie I purchased via YouTube. Times may vary slightly depending on what format or which edited version you are watching.

- **Continuity** - Neal checks his airline ticket, which shows that he departs from JFK airport. But the movie claims to have him flying out of LaGuardia. And that is also where those scenes were shot. (0:01:04 -0:01:08)

- **Continuity** - When the boss puts his hands on the table (0:01:39) they are spread wide. He removes his glasses with his left hand and brings that hand closer to the middle of the table (0:01:44). In the next cut his right hand goes from being spread far to being closer to the middle of the table as well (0:01:45).

- **Factual** - When Neal is trying to catch a cab to LaGuardia at about 5:30 PM in New York, it's still daylight. In reality, it would be after sunset by that time of day. The sun sets at about 4:30 that time in November.

- **Continuity** - When Neal races Kevin Bacon for the taxi, as he gets close to the cab all lanes of traffic are at a complete standstill. (0:03:46 - 00:03:48) Seconds later, when he trips over Del's trunk, the lane he falls into is empty and a car brakes hard to avoid hitting him. (0:03:51) The braking is an indication that it was travelling at a relatively high speed, which would have been impossible based on the previous shot.

- **Continuity** - In the scene where Neal trips over the trunk and falls into the street, the car that almost runs him over is a BMW. When it cuts to show Kevin Bacon's character getting into the taxi, the car that almost struck Neal is now a Lincoln Oldsmobile. (0:03:50 - 0:03:57).

- **Continuity** - As Neil is chasing the cab that Del stole, the bags he is carrying change hands in different shots. As he takes off after the cab (0:05:19) the brief-case is in his right hand. In the next cut showing him running toward the camera (0:05:20), the briefcase is in his left hand. Then two cuts later, it's back in his right hand (0:05:35).

- **Continuity** - As Neal's family is eating dinner, Neal Jr. (the boy who says "But I prefer noogies") is holding a fork in his right hand (0:06:47). When the camera cuts, the fork is on the table (0:06:48).

- **Continuity** - When Del pulls out his wallet and shows his shower curtain rings to Neal, Del's yellow shirt sleeve is pulled out and covering much of his wrist and watch (0:10:16). When it cuts to the close-up on his wallet, his watch and wrist are fully visible (0:10:18). In the next shot the sleeve again covers his watch and wrist (00:10:19).

- **Factual** – Shortly after Neal gets off the phone with his wife Susan, and Del comes over to chat with him, an airport announcement is heard in the background. When the female voice says for "Mary Ellen" to meet her party upstairs (0:12:49 – 0:12:54), there's a slight problem with that. There is no upstairs in the Wichita airport.

- **Continuity** – When they are sitting outside the Braidwood Inn, Neal tells Del that he has a Visa Card, a gasoline card and a Neiman Marcus Card. However, the night before when they checked into the motel, Neal paid with a Diners Club International card. (In 2004, Diners Club partnered with Mastercard in North America)

- **Continuity** - When Owen first arrives, he is wearing gloves on both hands (0:33:15). When he adjusts his hat (0:33:39), the right hand still has a glove on it. As he introduces himself and shakes their hands, Owen's right hand is now bare even though there wasn't enough time to remove the glove (0:33:45-0:33:49).

- **Factual** - When Owen is shaking Neal's hand, a Jay's Potato Chip truck drives by on the highway behind them. (0:33:50). Jay's is a local potato chip company out of Chicago, Illinois. Jays Potato Chips were not sold west of the Mississippi at the time.

- **Factual** - There is a mountain visible behind Owen. There are no mountains in Kansas

- **Blooper** - During the "sped-up" shot of the kid on the bus running up and down the aisles it appears that the kid's elbow or windmill accidentally struck the woman in the front left seat. If you look closely, you'll notice her eyes open in surprise as her head is struck (0:39:43).

- **Continuity** – As Del leads the bus in singing the theme music for *The Flintstones*, Neal's top button goes from unbuttoned (0:41:27), to buttoned (0:41:30), and then unbuttoned again (0:41:33).

- **Factual** - When Del and Neal are travelling from Jefferson City, Missouri to St.

Louis they are seen crossing the Mississippi River to enter downtown St. Louis.
This would not have been possible unless the bus driver overshot the entire
city and ended up across the river in Illinois. (0:41:37 — 0:41:46)

• **Continuity** - When Neal is scanning the
parking spaces in the rental car lot near
the airport, the shot switches to Neal's
POV and back again. When the camera
is on Neal, he walks past the Mercury
Sable in stall V-2; yet when it switches
back to his POV he's only just beginning
to pass the same spot. As he approaches
V-3 in the POV shot, the camera switches again and he's now well past it.
(0:45:53-0:46:01)

• **Continuity** - After Del spins the car out
of control and Neal says, "It's getting
pretty hot in here, you oughta take your
parka off" (0:59:13), Del's coat is half-off.
The next shot you see them driving
away (00:59:18) and Del's parka is fully
on again.

- **Continuity** - After the close call of Del driving the wrong direction on the freeway, Neal pulls his fingers out of holes he pressed into the car's dashboard, and Del releases his grip of the steering wheel to reveal the top of it has been bent forward (0:01:49). The next shot that shows the steering wheel (1:07:04), then when Neal is pulling his hands off the hot, sticky melted wheel (1:07:08) and all remaining views of it afterward, show the wheel back to its normal shape.

- **Continuity** - When Neal and Del are drinking and talking in the El Rancho hotel room, Neal finishes a tiny bottle of gin (1:12:29) and then starts drinking a tequila Del throws to him (1:12:34). But when the two toast the wives, Neal has gin in his hand again (1:13:38).

- **Continuity** - Shortly after leaving the El Rancho hotel in the morning, Neil seems to find some new clothes, including a too small red hunting hat and a scarf (1:16:19).

- **Continuity** – When the State Trooper tracks Del and Neal's burned car on his radar then pulls after them (1:16:47 - 1:16:59) it is a clear and sunny day. When it cuts to Del and Neal as they hear the siren, (1:17:00) their windshield wipers are active, and it appears to be snowing. Then the next cut showing the view of the trailing police car (1:17:02) reveals it's sunny and the road is dry.

- **Continuity** - When Del drives up in the passenger seat of the dairy truck, he is seen with a black eye (1:19:13-1:19:58). The black eye doesn't appear to be on his face when they are standing on the train platform in Chicago. But it's there again shortly after in the train station when he admits to being homeless. (1:23:53)

- **Continuity / Factual** - Neal leaves the Chicago subway station heading in a particular direction (for the sake of illustration, let's call that direction North). The train pulls into the station (1:20:55), Neal gets onto it, and it pulls away, heading North. (1:21:48). After Neal is sitting on the train and starts putting the clues together in his head, then returns, there's a shot of the same train heading South on the exact same track (1:23:37). That is impossible and is actually a shot of the train leaving North but played in reverse. If you look closely, you can very briefly see a person in a red jacket walking backwards on the other side of the railing that has the red "The Sun Run" sign above that spot and to the left a bit (1:23:43).

- **Continuity** - As Neil returns to the train station where he left Del, gets off the train and goes into the station, it's not the same station he was at earlier. The background outside reflecting in the train car windows (1:23:46) and visible outside the interior Del is sitting in (1:23:51) shows houses and trees instead of the tall Chicago buildings that were visible in the previous shots.

- **Continuity** - As Del and Neal approach Neal's home, Neal is carrying a large suitcase, instead of the garment bag and brief case he had (1:25:06 - 1:25:28).

- **Continuity** - This one is partially a continuity issue but also a bit of a plot hole. After the car burns, and they arrive at the El Rancho motel, Neal only has $17.00 on him and nothing but melted credit cards. This forces him to give up his cash and his watch to help pay for the room. Del only has $2.00 and a cheap watch that doesn't work as a bribe. At this point in the movie, Neal and Del only have $2.00. However, when Neal invites Del into the room, so he doesn't freeze to death, they are eating Doritos and drinking mini bottles of liquor. Even back in 1987 Doritos and tray of mini bottles from the hotel fridge bar had to have cost more than $2.00. Later on, the two take the Chicago subway, with Neal taking the subway in two different directions. Where did they get the money for that? At the time, fares were $1.00 and transfers were $0.25. One might assume that both Neal and Del had CTA monthly passes, but Neal's wallet had been burned in the car fire.

A LITTLE TROUBLE ON THE HOME FRONT
An entire sub-plot of NEAL's marriage woes mostly cut from the film

There are a few scenes in the movie where, when Neal is on the phone with his wife Susan, there seems to be some underlying tension that goes beyond his being "late" in returning home for Thanksgiving.

That's because there was an entire sub-plot that ended up being cut from the movie, related to some actual "troubles on the home front."

Those details are evident in the earlier drafts of the "Final Shooting Script" dated June 23, 1987, as well as an even earlier one dated May 22, 1986.

In the scene where Neal and his colleague John are finally released from the conference room with the indecisive chairman, there is a bit of dialogue that sets this up. Some of which stayed in the film. The following is from the June 1987 script.

NEAL
You're not going to the airport?

JOHN
What's the point of breaking your balls rushing for a six o'clock plane? Why don't you go out with me on the eight fifteen?

NEAL
I promised Susan I'd be home by nine.

JOHN
What difference does a couple of hours make?

NEAL
Under normal circumstances, none. But considering the state of affairs at the house these days, it makes all the difference.

JOHN
The six is a pain in the ass. Call and tell Susan it was delayed.

NEAL
I can't make that one work anymore.

That same scene, in the May 22, 1986, script, sets it up in a way to confirm that Neal is not an unfaithful man, but that there are stresses related to Neal's work, and, if anything, his "mistress" is his work.

NEAL
You're not going to the airport?

JOHN
I'm going out in the morning. No way I'm
breaking my nuts rushing for a plane
tonight. Why don't you hang with me and
we'll fly out tomorrow?

NEAL
You can pull that with your wife. I can't. If
I'm not home tonight, the marriage is a
historical fact. It's going to be bad enough
getting along with a household of relatives
but if we're fighting, it's gonna be hell.

JOHN
What's the difference if you're home at nine
tonight or nine tomorrow morning?

NEAL
To Susan, failure to meet one's scheduled
arrival time is a sure sign of marital
infidelity.

JOHN
She doesn't trust you?.

NEAL
Does your wife trust you?

JOHN
No. But I screw around. You don't.

NEAL
My mistress is a line of women's cosmetics.

JOHN
If it's that bad, you better split and you
better sit down and decide how you're going
to free up some time for the family. A bad
marriage eats time like you and me eat
peanuts.

Later that same day when Neal calls
from the New York airport, the dialogue
between the two of them is thick with
continued tension.

Parts of this scene also made it into the
final film.

INT. KITCHEN. EVENING

Bright and warm. A two-year old boy, SETH, is in
a highchair. At the kitchen table are a four year-old
boy, LITTLE NEAL, a seven year old girl, MARTI
and NEAL's wife SUSAN. She's in her mid-
thirties, attractive and strong. She gets up to answer
the phone.

SUE
(to Seth)
Keep your fingers out of Marti's food.
(Marti)
You keep your tongue in your mouth.

LITTE NEAL

I didn't do anything, did I?

                    SUE
No. You're waiting until I get on the phone.
(picks up the phone)
Hello?

Her cheery demeanor evaporates.

                    MARTI
Whom is it?

                    SUE
Where are you?

                    MARTI
Whom is it?

                    SUE
(to Marti)
Shh! It's Daddy.

Marti knows immediately what the conversation is
about. She informs her siblings.

                    MARTI
Flight delay.

INT. AIRPORT. NIGHT

Neal's on the pay phone. A couple of other men are
making the same call.

                    NEAL
You're not going to believe what happened .
. .

INT. KITCHEN. SUE. EVENING

She knows exactly what happened.

> SUE
> (fast, certain and sarcastic)
> You raced to the airport, nearly killed
> yourself and when you got to the gate the
> flight was delayed.

CU. NEAL.

His mouth is frozen open. She's stolen his words.

CU. SUE

She relents.

> SUE
> I know you can't prevent flight delays. You
> <u>can</u> prevent travelling immediately before a
> holiday. I asked you not to but you had your
> priorities.

CU. AIRPORT. NEAL. NIGHT

Neal rolls his eyes.

CU. SUE

She knows exactly what Neal's going to do

> SUE
> And don't roll your eyes.

INT. AIRPORT. NEAL

He's getting nowhere.

> NEAL
> Honey? I don't run the airline.

CU. SUE.

She doesn't like his attitude.

> SUE
> I'm not arguing on the phone. I'll see you
> when you get home.

She hangs up the phone.

After their plane is re-routed from Chicago to Wichita, there's a scene where Neal calls home to update Susan.

Like before, parts of this script made it into the final cut of the movie.

EXT. NEAL'S HOUSE. NIGHT

The snow is piling up. A TELEPHONE RINGS OVER.

INT. HOUSE. FOYER. NIGHT

It's dark. We HEAR THE PHONE RINGING.

INT. BEDROOM. NIGHT

Susan's asleep. She stirs, fumbles for the phone, answers.

SUSAN

Where are you?

INT. WITCHTA AIRPORT. CORRIDOR. NIGHT

Neal's on a pay phone

NEAL

Why am I in Witchita? Because we couldn't land in Chicago.

INT. NEAL'S HOUSE. BEDROOM. NIGHT

Susan's in bed. She's angry.

SUSAN

I don't understand what Witchita has to do with a snow storm in Chicago. Is there something going on, Neal?

INT. AIRPORT. DEL

He's sitting in a departure lounge, smoking, watching Neal.

HIS POV

Neal's across the corridor, talking on the phone.

CU. DEL

He studies Neal.

CU. NEAL

He continues his conversation.

> NEAL
> I'm doing the best I can. I'll be home as
> soon as possible. I have a key, I'll let myself
> in. Maybe if you're really lucky, the plane'll
> go down.

INT. HOUSE. BEDROOM. NIGHT

Susan resents the remark.

> SUSAN
> That's a real nice thing for a father to say. If
> you're coming home with an attitude, I'd
> rather you didn't come home at all. And I
> don't mean that in a mortal sense. Good
> night.

She hangs up the phone. In frustration, she socks
her pillow. She turns off the lights and buries
herself in the covers.

INT. AIRPORT. NEAL. NIGHT

He hangs up the phone, curses under his breath and
starts down the corridor. Del calls to him.

> DEL
> Neal?

Neal stops and turns. Del gets up from his seat and
shuffles into the corridor.

                    DEL
    A little trouble on the home front?

As far as Neal's concerned, his home life is none of
Del's business.

                    DEL
    Sounded like things were getting a little
    testy.

                    NEAL
    I don't think that's any of your concern.

                    DEL
    Probably not. I thought you might want to
    air some feelings.

                    NEAL
    I don't.

That same, scene, in the May 1986 version of the script, doesn't include the description, nor the dialogue between Susan
and the children.

INT. AIRPORT - CORRIDOR

Neal's on a pay phone.

                    NEAL
    Why am I in Wichita? Because we couldn't
    land in Chicago?
                    (pause)

I <u>know</u> it's snowing. That's why we couldn't land.
> (pause)

I have no idea. All the airlines said was we're refueling and continuing on to Chicago. They're probably lying but what else can I do?

INT. AIRPORT—DEL

He's in a flight lounge, sitting, smoking, watching Neal.

HIS POV

Neal's across the corridor, talking on the phone.

C.U. DEL

He yawns.

NEAL

He looks at his watch and wraps up the conversation

> NEAL
> It's quarter to eleven. Get back to sleep. I'll be fine. I have a key. You go to sleep. Okay. I love you. Okay. Bye.

He hangs up the phone. He curses under his breath and starts back down the corridor. Del calls to him.

There's a scene in the Braidwood, which was cut from the film, but did make it into one or more of the trailers released for the film, related to the pizza arriving at the hotel.

In that scene, the pizza boy doesn't have change for the hundred-dollar bill Del has, so, because Neal's in the shower, he searches Neal's stuff to find his wallet and pay the pizza delivery boy with a twenty he finds there.

(*The pizza boy, BTW, is the character who later sneaks into the hotel room while Del and Neal are sleeping, to steal the cash he previously saw was there*).

In a cut part of the conversation while the two are later in bed, that comes up. Part of Neal's dialogue that opens this scene also made it into one of the trailers for the film.

While the mention of the "skin magazines" Neal is traveling with is a subtle/small element, it could be a hint related to the sub-plot of the distance between Neal and Susan and Neal's loneliness.

NEAL

I was on my way home to spend a nice
holiday with my family and instead I'm in a
motel bed with a stranger five hundred
miles away from my house and I don't
know how or when I'll get there. I'm a
patient man. I'm paying for the room. I paid
for the cab…

DEL

You paid for the pizza, too.

NEAL

I did?

DEL

All I had was a hundred. The kid didn't
have change.

NEAL

You went in my wallet?

DEL

Are you mad?

NEAL

You have no right to go in my wallet!

DEL

What was I supposed to do? I had to pay for
the pizza. You were showering. Did you
want me to send some punk kid in to look at
your dick?

NEAL

You stay out of my stuff.

                    DEL
                (offended)
I'm not interested in your stuff.

                    NEAL
Good.

                    DEL
In fact, I'm bored with your stuff.

                    NEAL
What? You looked?

                    DEL
I didn't look

                    NEAL
Then why are you bored with it?

                    DEL
                (lying)
It's a figure of speech.

                    NEAL
Bullshit! You went through my bags!

Del jumps on the defensive.

                    DEL
How did I know you weren't some kind of
shady guy? I'm not sleeping with a stranger
without knowing a little about him. What if
you had a gun in your bag? I been on the
road too long to not know to take a
precaution or two.

NEAL
Did I go through your stuff?

DEL
I don't know. Did you?

NEAL
No, I did not! And I'm mad as hell that you
went through mine.

DEL
Two suits, two dirty shirts, some stale shorts
and some skin magazines.

Neal's embarrassed.

DEL
Don't sweat it, Neal. There's a reason every
hotel newsstand sells those kinds of
magazines. There isn't a married man alive
that hasn't…

NEAL
You done with your goddam cigarette?

Del takes one last puff. He drops it in a beer can
and swishes it out

DEL
Done.

Neil turns off the light.

The next morning, when Neal is talking to Susan on the phone, there's an entire section of their dialogue that didn't make it into the final cut of the film.

(*There is also, in this scene. a cut element from the film where Del had taken it upon himself to get Neal's suit laundered and starched. Because of it, Neal is forced to wear his clothes from the previous day. This leads to, later on, Del attesting to the fact that Neal has been wearing the same underwear since Tuesday.*)

INT. KITCHEN. DAY

Susan's in her robe, making school lunches, talking on the phone.

SUSAN

You shared a motel room with a stranger? Are you crazy?

INT. MOTEL ROOM. DAY

Neal's dressing as he talks. He removes a suit from a laundry box. It's gray wool.

NEAL

What was I supposed to do? Sleep in the airport?

SUSAN'S VOICE

This whole thing is insane. I don't know
what the hell you're doing!

NEAL
I'm trying to get home!

INT. KITCHEN. DAY

Susan pours herself another cup of coffee.

SUSAN
It doesn't sound like you're trying to get
home if you're shacking up with strangers.

INT. MOTEL ROOM. DAY

Neal slips on his shirt. He doesn't notice that the
sleeves are four inches too short.

NEAL
I didn't feel like sleeping in a chair.

SUSAN'S VOICE
I watched the news this morning and they
said O'Hare is open and flights are landing
and taking off.

Neal slips on his trousers. They're also four inches
too short. He doesn't notice.

NEAL
If that's the case, then I'll start trying to
book a flight.

SUSAN'S VOICE

It'd be nice if you could drop in for
Thanksgiving.

Neal slips on his suitcoat. It's also too short. He
turns to the mirror. Freezes. The phone falls out of
his hand to the floor.

At the St. Louis bus station restaurant,
shortly after Del has sold a bunch of his
shower curtain ring samples as earrings.

>   DEL
> Did you call the wife?

>   NEAL
> No one was home. They're probably at my
> daughter's Thanksgiving pageant.

>   DEL
> It's a bitch you missed it, huh? Those
> moments are precious.

Neal is coming to a realization. Something he's
known for awhile but hasn't admitted to.

>   NEAL
> I've been spending too much time away
> from home.

As Neal and Del are leaving St. Louis in
their rental car, there's a scripted scene
that didn't make it to the film of Susan

and the family, including her parent's and Neal's parents after their daughter's Thanksgiving pageant performance.

This long scene digs further into the sub-plot of the tension between Neal and Susan, with a major reveal and increased stakes in Neal and Susan's relationship implying she might have a good reason to be suspicious that he is having an affair. This scene also incorporates how others in the family feel about Neal's regular absences.

INT. NEAL'S HOUSE. DINING ROOM

Both sets of grandparents, the kids and Susan are having dinner. Susan is sullen and withdrawn, paying only cursory interest to the conversation.

> MARTIN
> I thought Marti did a wonderful job with her poem today.

> WALT
> It's a shame your Dad missed it

> JOY
> (sharply)
> I'm sure he feels the same way, Walt.

> SUSAN
> He'll see the video tape.

                    WALT
That's no way to watch a kid grow up.

Joy fires Walt a cold look to shut him up.

                    PEG
I was so proud of you, Marti.

                 LITTLE NEAL
Grandma, she missed about eight words.

                    MARTI
I did not!

                    SUSAN
That's enough.

                 LITTLE NEAL
She brutalized a famous poem.

The phone RINGS O.C. Susan slips away from the
table.

INT. KITCHEN

Susan walks into the kitchen and answers the
phone.

                    SUSAN
Hello?

INT. ROADHOUSE. PAY PHONE. NEAL

Neal's on the pay phone in a loud, raucous
roadhouse. Behind him we see a stage with a GIRL

dancing behind a shower curtain. A packed house cheers her on. Neal has his hand pressed against his ear.

> NEAL

Susan?

INT. NEAL'S HOUSE. KITCHEN, SUSAN

Susan hears the noise in the background.

> SUSAN

Where are you?

INT. ROADHOUSE. NEAL

He strains to hear. Del works his way through the crowd to the phone.

> NEAL

Huh?
> (pause)
I'm at a pay phone! What? Some roadside dump. I'm in Southern Illinois.

Del reaches Neal. He taps his shoulder. Neal looks around at him.

> NEAL
> (to Susan)

Hold on.

He covers the phone.

> DEL

Do you have five bucks?

NEAL
I'm on with my wife.

DEL
I need a five.

Neal reaches into his pocket and pulls out the last of the money.

NEAL
We only have twenty three bucks left.

DEL
We're fine. Give me five.

Neal fishes out a five.

DEL
Everything okay at home?

NEAL
You gotta be kidding.

Del turns.

NEAL
As soon as I'm off the phone, we're outta here.

Del looks back and gives him the okay.

INT. KITCHEN

Neal comes back on the line.

SUSAN
I'm sitting here with my parents, with <u>your</u>
parents, your kids, and I want to know
what's going on.

INT. ROADHOUSE. NEAL

He squeezes into the corner to shield the phone
from the noise.

NEAL
What's going on? I'm trying to get home.
I've had the worst day of my life. I've been
on a train that caught fire, a bus, the back of
a pick-up truck, I walked four miles through
the snow with four hundred people...

SUSAN'S VOICE
All I know is, John got home last night.

Neal's mouth drops open.

NEAL
He left after I did. How could he get home?

SUSAN'S VOICE
You tell me. The airport's been open since
this morning.

INT. KITCHEN

NEAL'S VOICE
You want to hear a dog story?

SUSAN
(to Martin)

He's not making any sense.

Martin takes the phone.

MARTIN

Neal? It's Dad.

INT. ROADHOUSE. NEAL

Drops his anger, cheers up. Excited to hear from his Dad.

NEAL

Hey, Dad! How are you?

MARTIN'S VOICE

Pretty good. And yourself?

NEAL

I'm having a hell of a time getting home but other than that I'm doing alright. When did you guys get in?

MARTIN'S VOICE

This morning.

NEAL

Did you hit any snow?

MARTIN'S VOICE

A little bit. The storm was pretty much just Chicago and north. Other than that it was pretty smooth sailing.

NEAL

Glad to hear it.

INT. KITCHEN

Martin covers the phone.

> MARTIN
> He's making perfect sense. What're you
> talking about?

Susan takes the phone.

INT. ROADHOUSE. NEAL

Continues talking.

> NEAL
> Dad? You have to help me out a little. I
> don't think Susan believes a word I'm
> saying.

INT. KITCHEN
Susan's jaw clenches.

> SUSAN
> You got that one right.

INT. ROADHOUSE. NEAL

His eyes open wide with alarm

INT. ROADHOUSE

Del looks over at the phone booth.

HIS POV

Neal lowers the phone and bangs his head on the wall.

INT. KITCHEN

Susan has dispatched the last of her patience.

> SUSAN
> I have a pretty good idea of what you're pulling, Neal, and all I can say is your timing stinks.

> NEAL'S VOICE
> I'm pulling something? I'm trying to get home however I can.

> SUSAN
> (bitter smile)
> How's Del.

INT. ROADHOUSE. NEAL

Neal doesn't understand what she's getting at.

> NEAL
> How's Del?

> SUSAN'S VOICE
> How's Del?

> NEAL
> Why do you want to know about Del? He's fine. A pain in the ass but why do you want to know about him?

INT. KITCHEN

Susan flashes a look into the dining room and then let's Neal have it.

> SUSAN
> You just better make sure you don't come home with <u>his</u> panties in your briefcase.

INT. ROADHOUSE. NEAL

Neal vastly misinterprets the remark.

> NEAL
> (with a smile)
> Funny you should mention that. I dried off my face with them this morning.

INT. ROADHOUSE. NEAL

Neal listens to the dial tone.

> NEAL
> Hello? Susan?
> (pause)
> Shit!

EXT. BOOTH. NIGHT

Neal rests his head on the cold glass and hangs up the phone.

In another scene that was cut entirely from the film, at one point in their long night-time highway drive in the rental car, shortly after the "you play with your balls a lot" scene, the two men stop at a cafe.

This scene reveals not only more about the stress in Neal's marriage, but a little more about Del, including the advice he offers that goes well beyond the previous "like your work, love your wife" motto that he previously shared.

INT. CAFÉ. NIGHT

Del and Neal are finishing their coffee.

> DEL
> If you want, I'll drive for a while.

> NEAL
> That's generous of you considering I've done most of the driving.

> DEL
> An hour behind the wheel with my back is like a lifetime for you.

Neal grows weary of the bickering. He changes the subject. To what's really bothering him.

> NEAL
> I can't believe it's Thanksgiving eve and I'm not home with my family.

> DEL

Me either.

NEAL
What do you have? Boys or girls?

DEL
(after a pause)
Two boys and a girl.

NEAL
I saw your wife. You got pictures of the kids?

DEL
In the trunk.

NEAL
It's hard being away, isn't it?

DEL
Absolute misery.

NEAL
I haven't seen you call your wife. Isn't she gonna worry?

DEL
Just because you didn't see me, doesn't mean I didn't call her.

NEAL
What's she have to say about all this?

DEL
Complete understanding.

NEAL

You're a lucky man. My wife's ready to kill me.

DEL

That's a shame. A real, true shame.

NEAL

I don't know what I can do. How do you manage to keep your wife so understanding?

DEL

It's real simple. I love her from sun-up to sundown and I make damn sure I don't leave her sight until I'm convinced she knows it. Marriage can be a pretty flexible institution if the two parties involved know without a doubt that the love they give will never be less than the love they receive. It sounds like a load of cornball crap but it works like magic

NEAL

Sounds like you have something pretty special.

DEL

We all have it at the start. Some people just lay it down while they're reaching for other things and when they miss it and go back for it, sometimes they don't remember where they left it.

Neal is silent as he considers Del's speech. Del finishes his coffee.

There is a line of dialogue cut from the motel scene, where Neal is trying to check in with credit cards that are burnt to a crisp. While most of the rest of the scene and dialogue appears in the film, there's a telling line as Neal pleads with the clerk.

CLERK
We need a major credit card.

NEAL
I don't have one. I'm tired. I'm cold, I'm humiliated, my marriage is collapsing, I'm two hundred miles from home on Thanksgiving Eve, my car burned up, I have been insulted, abused, assaulted and robbed. Please have mercy. I've been wearing the same undershorts for three days!

After Neal checks in to the hotel post-bribing the clerk with $17 and his expensive watch, there's a scene where he lifts the phone receiver, puts it to his ear and tries to dial.

But the rotary dial is locked.

He puts the phone down, sits for a moment, then goes to the window and sees Del sitting outside.

In the film, it cuts to Del's point of view. But in the final script, it cuts back to

Neal's home a few times and a dialogue between Susan and Peg, her mother-in-law.

PEG
That has nothing to do with his being stranded.

SUSAN
He's not stranded, Mother. Quit being so optimistic. He's fallen in love, he's trapped between me and the kids and someone else. He didn't call tonight because he's scared to tell me the truth.

PEG
That's absurd.

SUSAN
Is it?

PEG
Of course it is

SUSAN
Does anything he's said on the phone over the past two days make sense?

Peg doesn't answer.

SUSAN
The airport's open, the highways are clear, everything's back to normal and where's Neal? Stuck on the road with a salesman? Can you imagine Neal spending three seconds with this character he's described?

If he's going to invent someone, for God's
sake, he didn't have to go as far from reality
as he has.

PEG
Maybe he's embellished it a bit, but…

SUSAN
A bit? Marti comes up with more plausible
characters in her nightmares. If Neal wanted
to be home, he'd be home. He has money,
he has credit cards. There's no good reason
he's not here. Except…

PEG
I refused to believe that Neal would do
anything you're suggesting.

SUSAN
You just don't want to believe it. He doesn't
love me. I know it. I accept it. I'm going to
put on my best front, give the kids as warm
and loving a holiday as I can, then Friday
morning, we're gone.

[*The script cuts back to the motel where Neal and
Del are. Then it cuts back to Neal's house*]

She stands, picks up her tea cup, takes it to the sink
and crosses to the door.

SUSAN
He paid for the house, it's his and he can
share it with his darling Del.

She exits into the dark dining room.

[The script cuts, again, to the motel. Neal is in bed; He can't relax and gets back up to look out the window. In the script here he says: "What did I do to get hooked-up with that oaf?" And that's when it cuts to Del's monologue to Mari. Shortly after, when it's clear that Neal has invited Del in, the two philosophize about life and work. In that scene, Neal reveals a bit of his recent growth.]

NEAL

Money's no measurement of worth. True worth. Worth to the human race. I know because I have a lot of it and don't feel like I'm worth anymore than when I <u>was</u> broke. In fact I probably felt better about myself when I was broke.

[A few lines of dialogue later in that scene Neal says a line that did make it into the film: "At the very least, at the absolute minimum, you have a woman you love to grow old with."]

In a scene that is in the script but didn't make it to the final cut, after it's revealed that after being arrested by the State Trooper, Neal was strip searched and likely been given a cavity search, Del explains to Neal that he didn't get insurance on the rental car, and Neal punches Del in the face. (This explains the "blooper" where Del is spotted at a few scenes in this part of the film, with a black eye)

INT. COFFEE SHOP. DAY

Del's holding an ice cube wrapped in a napkin to his eye. Neal shuffles over to the booth and sits down.

> DEL
> You know this is twice in less than twenty four hours that you've slugged me

> NEAL
> I just called my wife and you'll be happy to know she hung up on me.

> DEL
>
> Oh, no.

Del lowers the ice cube.

> NEAL
> She didn't believe a word I said.

> DEL
> I'll be happy to confirm anything you'd like with her.

> NEAL
> Dinner hits the table right after the football game

He looks at the wall clock.

> NEAL
> Right now, it's eleven fifteen.

DEL

Let's pray for double overtime.

NEAL

I have a house full of family, a wife that's
ready to kill me…

DEL

Neal, I'm going to step up to this challenge.

NEAL

Please don't.

DEL

No, I am. I'll have to have you home before
the bird's out of the oven.

He gets up from the booth.

NEAL

Del, I'm begging you to sit down and leave
the situation alone.

DEL

What can happen? You get home. Or you
don't. Isn't it worth one last shot?

NEAL

No. Things are bad enough. Leave it alone.

DEL

Neal, you've hit the rock bottom. It doesn't
get much lower than having a state trooper
shine a flashlight up your can.

This next scene, which did not make it to the film occurs after the one where Del explains to Neal about Marie having been dead for eight years and that Del no longer has a home and lives on the road.

The script version you see below is compiled of a combination of the May 22, 1986, and the June 23, 1987, scripts.

INT. KITCHEN. NIGHT

Neal's wife, SUE, is finishing a relish tray. Her mother, JOY, is stirring gravy. And her mother-in-law, PEG, is whipping mashed potatoes with an egg beater.

                    SUE
For all I know, Neal could be splattered all over some highway somewhere.

Peg shuts off the egg beater. It's her son.

                    PEG
Are you just trying to upset me?

                    JOY
Of course not.
                    (to Sue)
Last time he called he said what?

                    SUE
He said he and this Del Griffith person were in Oconomowoc, Wisconsin…

PEG
Martin and I have friends in Oconomowoc,
the Kidner's. Their boy's a state trooper.

SUE
I think he's full of crap. He said the rental
car burned up. He said he got robbed. He
and this Del Griffith.

JOY
Who's Del Griffith?

SUE
Some guy he met at the airport in New
York.

Sue stops her work.

PEG
The airport was closed, honey. I don't know
how you expect him to get in when the airport's closed.

SUE
He was with Jerry Lane in New York. I
called Jean Lane this morning. She said Jerry left New York Tuesday morning. A day
later than Neal, and he's home, so don't tell
me he couldn't get home!

She undoes her apron and throws it down on
the table. She storms out of the room

JOY
Oh, boy.

                    PEG
Neal wouldn't lie to her.
                    (pause)
Would he?

Neither the May nor the June scripts I
was able to find have any other resolution
to the marital woes than Neal and Del
coming through the front door. But the
fact Neal is with a man named Del Griffith is likely enough for Susan to realize
he was not lying and all of the misadven-
tures and wild stories he'd been sharing
with her were actually the truth.

And in the May 1986 version of the
script, the following, which is pretty close
to the final cut of the film, appears.

INT. HOUSE—TOP OF THE STAIRS

Susan's at the top of the stairs, looking down. Her
eyes are darkened with mascara moistened by her
tears. She sniffles and composes herself

INT. FOYER – NEAL

He looks past Seth to the stairs and sees Susan. He
smiles from rim to rim.

NEAL
   Honey? I'd like you to meet a friend of
   mine

Del looks up the stairs. He pushes his mussed hair
back and smiles humbly.

C.U. SUSAN

She smiles.

SUE
   Hello, Mr. Griffith.

INT. FOYER.

Neal gives Seth to Del and charges up the stairs.
Susan runs down and they embrace mid-way. Neal
kisses her like never before.

That clench and kiss between Neal and
Susan, and the touching smile on Del's
face is how the film ends.

And I'm not sure about you, but I can't
watch that scene, or even think about it,
without my eyes starting to moisten.

A TALE OF TWO JOHNS
With THANKS to
John Candy & John Hughes

While so many people make up the cast and crew of the movie (Steve Martin, Laila Robins, Michael McKean, Kevin Bacon, Dylan Baker, Edie McClurg, just to name a few), I couldn't compile this book without a special nod of thanks and appreciation to John Hughes and John Candy.

And that's why I'm sharing extremely brief biographies for them here. I strongly encourage you to read more from the many other books that document and share details about both of their lives and their legacies. I list a few of them in the resources and further readings section at the end of this book.

John Candy

Born on October 31, 1950, in Newmarket, Ontario, Canada, John Franklin Candy was a Canadian actor known mainly for his roles in comedy movies.

While studying journalism at both Centennial College and McMaster University, Candy discovered his love of acting. He was cast in several smaller film and television productions in the early 1970s and became a member of the Toronto branch of the improvisational group The Second City in 1972.

SCTV (Second City Television), a Canadian sketch comedy show, which began in 1976 on Canadian television and later went on to air on both NBC and ABC in the United States, is where Candy's career started to take off.

Candy's roles in film included *Stripes*, *Splash*, *The Blues Brothers*, B*rewster's Millions*, *Volunteers* and *Spaceballs*. His first Hollywood lead roles came in *Summer Rental* and *Armed and Dangerous*.

Among many other roles, his collaborations with John Hughes included *Planes, Trains and Automobiles*, *National Lampoon's Vacation*, *Uncle Buck*, *She's Having a Baby*, *The Great Outdoors*, *Home Alone* and *Career Opportunities*.

In addition to many other roles in television, movies, and even music videos (he had cameos in Ray Parker's "Ghostbusters" and The Traveling Wilburys' "Wilbury Twist), Candy was a co-owner of the Canadian Football League (CFL) Toronto Argonauts. The team won the coveted Grey Cup under his ownership in 1991.

Candy died at the age of 43 from a heart attack in his sleep on March 4, 1994, while filming *Wagon's East*.

He is survived by his wife, Rosemary Hobor, children Christopher Michael and Jennifer Anne, and a grandchild.

John Hughes

John Wilden Hughes, Jr. was born on February 18, 1950, in Lansing Michigan as the only boy in a family with four children and has been described as a "quiet kid."

After deciding to leave the University of Arizona to pursue a career writing (humor and advertising copywriting), Hughes sold jokes to comedians such as Joan Rivers and Rodney Dangerfield. He was also responsible for creating the famous Edge "Credit Card Shaving Test" ad campaign. Hughes eventually worked as a regular contributor to *National Lampoon* magazine, and one of his first published stories, "Vacation '58" inspired by his own childhood family trips, became the basis for the movie *National Lampoon's Vacation*.

His first credited screenplay was *National Lampoon's Class Reunion*, and his directorial debut came with *Sixteen Candles*.

Movies about teenage life were a common theme with Hughes, and included *The Breakfast Club*, *Weird Science*, *Pretty in Pink*, *Ferris Bueller's Day Off*, and *Some Kind of Wonderful*.

In an effort to avoid being identified only as a maker of teen movies, Hughes released *Planes, Trains and Automobiles*, *She's Having a Baby*, *Uncle Buck* and *National Lampoon's Christmas Vacation*. Additional films included *Home Alone*, *Curly Sue*, *The Great Outdoors* and *Dennis the Menace*.

Hughes retired from the public eye in 1994, moving back to the Chicago area. While revisiting New York to see family, John Hughes died on August 6, 2009, of a heart attack while taking a walk.

His wife, Nancy, died in 2019. He is survived by his sons John Hughes III, James Hughes, and his grandchildren.

CONCLUSION

The round-about way I arrived at this book parallels the movie

The idea for this book has been with me for years and kept coming back to me almost every time I watched the movie.

But the version of this book that you just read wasn't the first concept I had.

Considering that the book Del Griffith is reading in that New York airport was a fictional title, I had the idea that the book I created as a nod to the movie should also be a work of fiction.

My original idea had been to create an anthology of short stories, asking the contributors to each submit a story in any genre with the title of "The Canadian Mounted." The only genre I did not want for this project would be erotica. That would be part of the joke—to have a title like that with not a single erotic story in it.

I wanted that anthology to also have a chapter at the end that included trivia and interesting anecdotes related to the movie.

But as the information and trivia I was gathering grew, combined with just how much work editing an anthology can be, the book, like the side-track journey Del and Neal engage in, took a different route.

I love the movie, and, though I've watched the special features on the DVD or Blu-ray Disc™ and other formats; read up on and watched as much as I could about the "behind the scenes" for the movie, I felt it would be worthwhile if there was a book that attempted to capture as many of those "extra" elements for fans of the movie as possible.

When I first put this book up for pre-order, I was pleasantly surprised to find that there were people, very much like me, who were huge fans of the book, who recognized that little paperback Del had been holding, and who were eager to get their hands on it.

I do hope, dear reader, that I did not disappoint, or let down a fellow fan of *Planes, Trains and Automobiles* and of all of the incredible people who made that movie happen.

And I hope this book enhances your future experiences re-watching a great film.

SOURCES & REFERENCES
And further reading

Here is a list of many of the resources used for gathering content and information compiled into this book. They were invaluable in my research.

For further reading, viewing, or listen-ing pleasure, I encourage you to check them out.

Books

- Clarke, Jamie. *Don't You Forget About Me: Contemporary Writers on the Films of John Hughes.* New York: Gallery Books, 2007.

- Diamond, Jason. *Searching for John Hughes: Or Everything I Thought I Needed to Know About Life I Learned from Watching '80s Mov-ies.* New York: HarperCollins, 2016.

- Fowke, Edith and MacMillan, Keith. *The Penguin Book of Canadian Folk Songs.* Har-mondsworth, 1973.

- Honeycut, Kirk. John Hughes: A Life in Film. New York: Race Point Publishing, 2015.

- Knelman, Martin. Laughing on the Outside: The Life of John Candy. New York: St. Mar-tin's Press, 2014.

- Leslie, Mark & Krishnasamy, Shayna. *Maca-bre Montreal: Ghostly Tales, Ghastly Events, and Gruesome True Stories*. Toronto: Dun-durn, 2018.

- Maltin, Leonard. *Leonard Maltin's Movie Guide*. New York: Signet Books, 2016.

- Morgan, Tracey, J. *Searching for Candy – John Candy: A Biography*. USA, 2019.

- Morgan, Tracey J. *Those Aren't Pillows: A Fan's Guide to Planes, Trains & Automobiles*. Seattle: Tracey J. Morgan, 2020.

Videos

- "John Hughes." YouTube, Iamthe80sguy2, August 22, 2014,
  https://www.youtube.com/watch?v=8JHQtj tPXDI

- "Heartbreak and Triumph: The Legacy of John Hughes." YouTube, Blu-ray Extras, August 8, 2018,
  https://www.youtube.com/watch?v=GaJPK ObElGo

- "John Hughes Tribute: 2010 Oscars." YouTube, Oscars, March 10, 2010,
  https://www.youtube.com/watch?v=DvmVY Nr0lk0

- "Getting There is Half the Fun: The Story of Planes, Trains and Automobiles" Special Feature on *Planes, Trains and Automobiles*
  (*"Those Aren't Pillows!" Edition*), Paramount DVD Video, 2009.

Articles

- Cormier, Roger. "15 Moving Facts About Planes, Trains and Automobiles." *Mental Floss*, November 22, 2017. https://www.mentalfloss.com/article/71594/1 4-moving-facts-about-planes-trains-and-automobiles

- M, Matt. "20 Things You Probably Never Never About Planes, Trains and Automo-biles." *Eighties Kids*, August 24, 2018. https://www.eightieskids.com/15-fascinating-facts-you-probably-never-knew-about-planes-trains-and-automobiles/

- Sweeten, Julia. "The House from the Movie 'Planes, Trains and Automobiles.'" *Hooked on Houses*, May 21, 2012. https://hookedonhouses.net/2012/05/21/plan es-trains-automobiles-house/

- Vannicola, Joe, "Interview with Debra Lamb." *A Joe's Eye View*, November 25, 2012. https://infosack.blogspot.com/2012/11/interv iew-with-debra-lamb.html

- Zinski, Dan. "Will Smith & Kevin Hart Star-ring in Planes, Trains & Automobiles Re-make." *Screen Rant*, August 17, 2020. https://screenrant.com/planes-trains-automobiles-movie-remake-will-smith-kevin-hart/

Misc. Online Resources

- "Planes, Trains and Automobiles." *IMDb*. https://www.imdb.com/title/tt0093748/

- "Planes, Trains and Automobiles." *Wikipe-dia*. https://en.wikipedia.org/wiki/Planes,_Trains_and_Automobiles

- "Carlyle Books (Compiled with Jerry Boyaj-ian)." *MOAM.INFO*. https://moam.info/carlyle-books-compiled-with-jerry-boyajian_5991a8ef1723ddd269e55175.html

- Morgan, Tracey J. "Things you may or may not know about Planes, Trains and Auto-mobiles..." *Searching for Candy: A blog about writing the book*. November 22, 2016. http://searchingforcandy.blogspot.com/2016/ 11/ things-you-may-or-may-not-know-about.html

- Tipton, Ken. "Part 3 – The Later Years." *Lost Valley - Lost Innocence: A Love Story By Ken Tipton*. https://www.lostvalley.movie/part-3-later-years

- u/cru_jonze, "In Deadpool 2, Wade is read-ing the same book John Candy reads in Planes, Trains and Automobiles." *Reddit*, September 25, 2018. https://www.reddit.com/r/MovieDetails/comments/9iv430/in_deadpool_2_wade_is_reading_the_same_book_john/

ABOUT THE AUTHOR

Mark's thirty years of experience working in the book industry started in 1992, the same year his first short story appeared in print. He has since published more than thirty books and continues to work as an industry representative and consultant.

When he is not quoting from classic John Hughes movies, Monty Python, or random song lyrics Mark can be found haunting local bookstores, libraries, and craft beer establishments.

You can find him online at www.markleslie.ca.

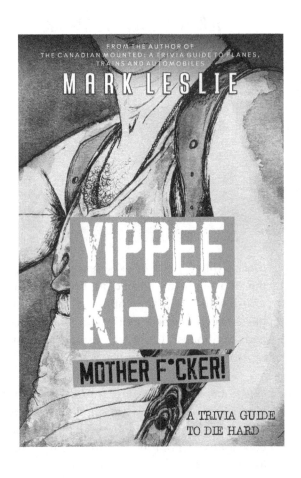

FROM THE AUTHOR OF
THE CANADIAN MOUNTED: A TRIVIA GUIDE TO PLANES,
TRAINS AND AUTOMOBILES

MARK LESLIE

YIPPEE
KI-YAY
MOTHER F°CKER!

A TRIVIA GUIDE
TO DIE HARD

IF YOU'RE LOOKING FOR MORE
1980s MOVIE NOSTALGIA /TRIVIA

WELCOME TO THE PARTY, PAL!

When Die Hard premiered in July 1988 John McClane didn't just become a fly in Hans Gruber's ointment, he heralded in a new era of action movies, inspired countless knock-off action movies best described as "Die Hard in a" or "Die Hard on a" copycats, and created a franchise that spanned five decades (if you include the 2020 DieHard battery commercial). Even thirty-five years later it continues to inspire heated annual debates regarding the film's status as a Christmas movie.

This guide, lovingly researched by a die-hard (pun completely intended) fan of the 1988 action-adventure blockbuster collects trivia, behind-the-scenes stories of the movie, the script, the actors, and the books and other written material that Die Hard and several of the follow-on films in the franchise were based on or inspired by.

SELECTED BOOKS

Non-Fiction ("Ghost Stories")

Macabre Montreal
Haunted Hospitals
Creepy Capital
Tomes of Terror
Spooky Sudbury
Haunted Hamilton

Fiction

The Canadian Werewolf Series
A Canadian Werewolf in New York
Stowe Away
Fear and Longing in Los Angeles
Fright Nights, Big City
Lover's Moon
Hex and the City

Evasion
I, Death
Active Reader: And Other Cautionary Tales from the Book World
Nocturnal Screams (Short Fiction Series)

Made in the USA
Las Vegas, NV
01 December 2023